# A Handbook for Leaders in Higher Education

Written to assist those seeking to understand the key global drivers, and an overview of key challenges facing senior leaders and managers today, this book focuses on the complex and highly politicised area of teaching and learning in higher education. Providing tried and tested tips and techniques for addressing the 'why, what and how' of leadership and management theory and practice, it is firmly grounded in the context of the teaching and learning arena. *A Handbook for Leaders in Higher Education: Transforming teaching and learning* can be dipped into to provide knowledge and understanding of theory, best practice examples, case study exemplars and reflective practice activity.

It is structured in four main parts:

- A view from the top
- The leadership and management perspective
- Engendering a change culture
- Looking to the future.

This handbook is informed by senior leaders and experts with expertise in delivering excellent practice in teaching and learning at international, national and institutional levels.

Responding to the need of universities to take the lead in changing cultures and working practices, this book is an essential and forward-looking text for both scholars and practitioners in the senior teams of higher education institutions.

**Stephanie Marshall** is Chief Executive of the Higher Education Academy (HEA), UK.

# A Handbook for Leaders in Higher Education

Transforming teaching and learning

**Stephanie Marshall**

 Routledge
Taylor & Francis Group

LONDON AND NEW YORK

First published 2016
by Routledge
2 Park Square, Milton Park, Abingdon, Oxon OX14 4RN

and by Routledge
711 Third Avenue, New York, NY 10017

*Routledge is an imprint of the Taylor & Francis Group, an informa business*

© 2016 Stephanie Marshall

*British Library Cataloguing in Publication Data*
A catalogue record for this book is available from the British Library

*Library of Congress Cataloging in Publication Data*
A catalog record for this book has been requested

ISBN: 978-1-138-90979-3 (hbk)
ISBN: 978-1-138-90980-9 (pbk)
ISBN: 978-1-315-69379-8 (ebk)

Typeset in Palatino
by Swales & Willis Ltd, Exeter, Devon, UK

Printed and bound in Great Britain by
Ashford Colour Press Ltd, Gosport, Hampshire

# Contents

# Case studies

# Case study contributors

**Professor Shirley Alexander**, Deputy-Vice-Chancellor and Vice-President (Education and Students), University of Technology, Sydney

**Professor Sir Richard Barnett**, Vice-Chancellor (recently retired), University of Ulster

**Chris Cox**, Director of Development, University of Manchester

**Geoff Dawson**, Chair of Governors, Sheffield Hallam University

**Professor Ian Dunn**, Deputy-Vice-President, Coventry University

**Stephen Gomez**, Pearson Education

**Professor Debra Humphris**, Vice-Chancellor, University of Brighton, formerly Vice Rector, Imperial College London

**Dr Tom Kennie**, Ranmore Consulting Group

**Professor Pauline E. Kneale**, Pro-Vice-Chancellor, Plymouth University

**Sir Alan Langlands**, Vice-Chancellor, University of Leeds

**Sue Littlemore**, former BBC Education Correspondent

**Dr Terry Maguire (Director) and Professor Sarah Moore (Chair)**, National Forum for the Enhancement of Teaching and Learning in Higher Education

**Professor Stephanie Marshall**, CEO, Higher Education Academy

**Professor Philip Martin**, Pro-Vice-Chancellor, Sheffield Hallam University

**Professor Peter Mathieson**, President, University of Hong Kong (UHK)

**Professor Robin Middlehurst**, Professor of Higher Education, Kingston University and Higher Education Academy

**Professor Tim Millar**, Vice-Provost, University of Arizona

**Jacqueline F. Moloney**, Chancellor, University of Massachusetts Lowell

**Anne Morrison**, formerly of the BBC

**Professor Anton Muscatelli**, Provost, University of Glasgow

**Professor David Phoenix**, Vice-Chancellor, London South Bank University (LSBU)

**Professor Sue Rigby**, Deputy-Vice-Chancellor, University of Lincoln (formerly University of Edinburgh)

**Professor Alistair Sambell**, Vice-Principal, Edinburgh Napier University

**Professor Tim Stewart**, Dean of the Business School, BPP Business School

**Professor Rolf Tarrach**, former President of University of Luxembourg, now President of European Universities Association (EUA)

**Christian Tauch**, German Rektors' Council

**Professor Amy B. M. Tsui**, Pro-Vice-Chancellor and Vice-President (Teaching and Learning), University of Hong Kong

**Professor Gilly Salmon**, Pro-Vice-Chancellor, University of Western Australia

**Steve Williams**, Director of University IT, Newcastle University

**Ewart Wooldridge**, CBE, Founding CEO of the Leadership Foundation for Higher Education

# Preface

This book recognises that university leadership is crucial to get a coherent focus on teaching and learning in higher education.

There is a real change in university priorities underway – and for several reasons. In the past the crucial metrics were about research – or the prior attainment of students. Now we are seeing a real effort to develop metrics which at least capture some aspects of the student's academic experience. Students are more aware that £9,000 is going in to their education and are rightly challenging universities to show that they are getting an education which is worth that amount. And ministers are rightly responding to this public concern by urging universities to focus on teaching quality.

These pressures however only lead to practical action if universities then take the lead in changing cultures and changing working practices. One survey a few years ago showed that when academic staff rated the factors that led to their promotion they placed research performance top, contribution of the departmental administration second and then teaching performance came in third. That dismal result was probably an accurate reflection of the reality of academic life in universities. I hope and believe it is slowly changing.

There were opportunities before. The Robbins report had detailed information on student contact hours and size of classes. Robbins worried that "in the making of appointments and promotion . . . . published work counts for too much in comparison with other kinds of excellence." (Robbins Report 1963. Paragraph 561) But nothing really changed then. Now there is a new opportunity. Graham Gibbs has shown the importance of student engagement and proposed some measures which are good proxies for that. Now Jo Johnson, the Minister for Universities is proposing a Teaching Excellence Framework to match – though not copy – the Research Excellence Framework.

The Higher Education Academy, led with distinction by Stephanie Marshall, has an important role here. It really can promote change in the lecture halls, laboratories and seminar rooms of our universities. Change does not have to come through the barrel of a gun. Our universities value their autonomy and academic staff expect to be treated with respect. The excellent case study contributors brought together in these pages offer good practical advice on what universities can do. I warmly welcome it.

**The Right Honourable Lord Willetts was Minister
for Universities and Science, 2010–2014**

# Acknowledgements

I would like to extend huge thanks to the many colleagues in the Higher Education Academy's pro-vice-chancellor network, who are always prepared to go the extra mile in their quest to continually improve the student learning experience and its leadership. An especial thanks to the case study contributors: their input makes this book really come alive. And finally, this book is for Ewart, whose friendship, insights and challenge have inspired me over many years.

# Introduction

## BACKGROUND

Ask any leader what the high spot of their career has been, and they will inevitably recount a story (or even stories!) of how they addressed a particular challenge, how they made sense of it, and, working with their staff, rose to meet it and move on. Leadership never takes place in a controlled environment. If it did, would not the role of the leader be rather dull, unchallenging and unfulfilling? Leadership of teaching and learning in the present climate offers some unprecedented opportunities which include: working in an environment which is a rich mix of cultural diversity, technological advances which have the potential to inspire and individualise student learning, and a political discourse about the fundamentals of teaching excellence. This introduction is divided into three parts. The first part provides a background, exploring drivers of the current agenda for teaching and learning in higher education (HE). The second part offers an overview of key results from a questionnaire administered to the executive leads with responsibility for teaching and learning across all the publicly funded universities of the UK, with their concerns generating the key themes to be addressed in this handbook. Finally, the last part provides guidance on how to use the handbook: who it is for, how it is organised and a summary of the key themes. These are covered in the eleven chapters which are grouped into four parts: (I) A view from the top, (II) The leadership and management perspective, (III) Engendering a change culture and (IV) Looking to the future.

## TEACHING AND LEARNING IN HE: THE CHANGING LEARNING LANDSCAPE

Since the 1970s, HE in developed countries has moved beyond an elite system to one that is more accessible and inclusive, and has therefore expanded enormously. At the time of writing, teaching and learning has risen to the top of both political and institutional agendas due to a combination of:

- recovery from the global recession;
- new and/or higher fees – or the absence of them, with higher fees at least in England dependent on successful engagement with a new **Teaching Excellence Framework (TEF)** to be introduced in 2016;
- concern for international competitiveness fuelled by the rapid rise of HE in the Far East;
- the promotion of students as 'global citizens'.

Globally, not only have the numbers of indigenous students increased within higher education institutions (HEIs), but also those from an international market. The growth in numbers of international students seeking undergraduate education outwith their own country has been particularly significant and important over the past twenty years. Competition between global universities to attract international students is intensifying not only between nations, but between institutions.

Listening to executive leaders of teaching and learning, one cannot help but be struck by how many of the challenges highlighted above have become translated into **key performance indicators (KPIs)** which these individuals are tasked to deliver. The role of these senior managers is to strategise and lead delivery on a complex range of fronts to include student access, home student recruitment, student retention, student progression, the **National Student Survey (NSS)** and international student recruitment. Indeed, reading any of the job descriptions for pro-vice-chancellors (PVCs), deputy-vice-chancellors (DVCs), vice-principals (VPs) or vice-presidents (VPs) holding portfolio responsibility for teaching and learning – a range of different titles for which I shall adopt the generic title of 'VP (Teaching and Learning)' – one cannot help but be amazed at the enormity of the role.

This leads to the question that has recently emerged in the UK (and, indeed, globally) about how best to support and develop these institutional leaders. The **Higher Education Academy (HEA)** – the national body tasked with supporting the sector with the delivery of an excellent student learning experience – has a network of VPs from across the UK. They meet twice yearly to network, engage with a range of issues such as learning spaces, student surveys, learning analytics, cutting edge thinking and contribute to a range of workshops to address their requirements. The content of these overnight 'retreats' is determined by two convenors chosen from the network, with rotation of representation every three years. In the autumn of 2013, one of the themes for discussion was 'Leadership of Teaching and Learning'. A number of VPs were concerned that the role was continually expanding. They wanted to explore how best the **HEA** could assist individuals to understand the rapidly changing policy landscape and how best to translate new policy into practice. (This concern was further complicated in the UK by growing differences of policy and practice across the four nations of England, Scotland, Wales and Northern Ireland). They also wanted to consider how best they could prepare the next cadre of executive leaders, addressing succession planning through consideration of the 'talent pipeline' – that is, heads of school, deans and various professional services staff working in the directorates offering support on a range of student matters.

These discussions prompted a number of actions for the **HEA**. The first was to nominate a serving VP to undertake a sample needs analysis of the areas where it was felt that the leadership of teaching and learning was proving to offer challenges beyond which individuals felt they were prepared. The majority of these staff had been on leadership programmes, but were now advocating a leadership of teaching and learning programme 'which would create space for policy development and debate', alongside 'developing a deeper understanding of learning and teaching … for world-leading curricula'. It was decided that, as a result of this sampling, the VP would report back to the next network meeting with suggestions. The result – reported back to the group in spring 2014 – was an overview of key areas where further training and development were deemed important and which constituted a coherent leadership development programme. Everyone wanted the programme to be embedded in the policy landscape, with an emphasis on a case-study approach of how different HE executive leaders had responded to this policy context and translated the key drivers into something meaningful and distinctive.

Floating the idea of the programme – for existing VPs but also, more particularly, for aspiring VPs so as to develop the talent pipeline – met with support. Concurrently, I responded to a request I had received from a number of people to write a text which covered the unique challenges of locating and conflating current best practice in leadership in the context of teaching and learning. It was clearly the appropriate time to assemble a handbook – *Leading teaching and learning* – which would provide a framework for reflection on policy and practice.

To gather further material to inform the handbook and the programme, it was decided to undertake a survey of all the VPs (Teaching and Learning) of the UK (approximately 160), to drill down into the areas that had been highlighted in the earlier sample interviews conducted to inform the new programme (with a response rate of 25 per cent). The emerging key themes are set out below and underpin the chapters and the points of emphasis in this book.

## WHAT EXECUTIVE LEADERS OF TEACHING AND LEARNING TELL US

> Within higher education institutions you have to battle with the attitude that 'it's learning and teaching so it doesn't count' which exists in all institutions regardless of standing or origin. I think you have to lead by example and be plausible – you have to have a fully rounded academic profile (engaged in research and learning and teaching) whereas a leader in research isn't expected in most institutions to demonstrate their scholarship in learning and teaching. You need a thick skin.
>
> (questionnaire respondent)

The origins of this book lie in my concern to change perceptions such as the one highlighted above. I have observed over the past five years that leadership of teaching and learning in HE in particular has become increasingly complicated due to a range of factors. They include: the acceleration of technological advances, global markets, financial constraints, greater concern for social justice and governments and ministries actively intervening in policy which invariably necessitate changed practice. VPs (Teaching and Learning) are the lynchpin of 'sense-making' of these ongoing changes. They are also essential in terms of translating them into practice – via carefully thought-through strategies – that will enhance the learning experience of their students. The key broad areas respondents flagged up as 'areas for development' included:

- governance (both at the **board** level and internally);
- working with and engaging others – without power or authority;
- conceptualising how best to lead major change projects.

The majority of the respondents to the survey of VPs had 'grown up' in an academic environment, although 46 per cent had entered HE further to careers in other public sector environments, most particularly the NHS. Fifty-two per cent cited previous experience of a role focused on teaching and learning as a reason for wishing to move into an executive role, leading institutional strategic developments. Forty-five per cent of PVCs had been heads of schools or deans prior to taking on their executive brief, with deans stating that they had experienced a greatening focus on teaching and learning when in that role. They all expressed a desire to gain more support in understanding and conceptualising – particularly via case study illustrations of best practice – how best to motivate and engage staff in this particularly crucial, core activity of their universities.

## PURPOSE OF THE HANDBOOK

As a consequence of the above, this book is aimed at those working in, or aspiring to work in top teams in HEIs. Roles include head of school, head of student services, head of quality units, deans, directors of student experience, etc. The primary purpose of the book is to be a handbook which will assist those looking for an overview of key issues facing senior leaders and managers in HE, alongside providing well-tried tips and techniques for addressing problems. As such, this handbook can be dipped into to support understanding and guide practice, through both theory and best practice examples and case studies derived primarily from the UK, but also from around the globe. This is not to say that the book cannot be read as a whole; indeed, a number of researchers into HE have welcomed the notion of such a book, suggesting that it is most timely and, most importantly, fills a void.

## ORGANISATION OF THE HANDBOOK

The underlying philosophy of the volume, which is divided into four parts, is to provide a useable and practical resource for senior leaders with responsibility for the strategic direction of teaching and learning.

Each chapter is written so that it can be read as a coherent whole so that those in leadership roles grappling with some of the issues concerning different aspects of leading teaching and learning can access (i) an overview of a key topic – the 'what'; (ii) consideration of key aspects to include tried and tested examples of best practice – the 'how'; and (iii) a summary of points to consider when tackling particular aspects. Additionally, each chapter provides opportunities to pause and interrogate one's own practice, read case study illustrations written by senior leaders from around the globe, and understand the terminology through the provision of a comprehensive glossary (with terms emboldened in the text defined). All the chapters are sensitive to the practicalities of mass HE in terms of size, resources, diversity and mission, and respect the international nature of the work we are involved in.

### Part I: A view from the top

This section explores the international and national drivers for change impacting on the agenda for teaching and learning in HE. It commences with an overview of changes and drivers causing nations to up their game, striving to deliver teaching excellence. Examples of two distinctive approaches are offered from Professors Sir Alan Langlands and Anton Muscatelli, illustrating their own distinctive institutional approaches. The section moves on to explore the critical role of governance and leadership in their response to these external drivers, and to define the role of VPs (Teaching and Learning). Finally, it considers how the contribution of academic leadership has been enhanced to offer role models that can serve to inspire best practice amongst everyone who is engaged in both constructing teaching activity and uplifting learner outcomes. The author underpins this by offering a new model of academic practice, 'structured improvisation'.

### Part II: The leadership and management perspective

This section flows from concern to enhance the skills of academic leadership, which has been highlighted as a key strategic issue for HE providers. Selecting and developing VPs (Teaching and Learning) has become an increasingly difficult task as the external environment becomes more complex, particularly the ever-changing learning landscape. Once a distributed leadership model is in place in an institution, team working and team building become essential to deliver holistic provision for students. Additionally, the role of performance management – at both the team and individual levels – is an important means by which progress against ambition can be monitored and addressed.

## Part III: Engendering a change culture

This section first looks at the national sector-level developments in three different nations. Each explores how to incentivise VPs (Teaching and Learning) to take up the baton of leading teaching excellence. It then focuses on the institutional level, providing two chapters which explore basic frameworks for leading, managing and transitioning change. Particular case-study examples of change cover developments in: curriculum, technology, learning spaces and promotions criteria to recognise leadership in teaching and learning.

## Part IV: Looking to the future

This section offers both external and personal reflections on what the future might hold. In such a rapidly changing landscape is it not better to try to shape the future than wait for it to be foisted on us? In the first chapter in this section, contributors examine what leaders of teaching and learning might have to contend with in the future, and what the key challenges might be. And, in the final chapter, the author presents her view of the future, highlighting three challenges that we need to address now, if we are really serious about empowering each and every student to make their own unique contribution to society.

Finally, it leaves me to welcome you, the reader, and invite you to read on, reflect on your own practice and how it can be enhanced, and, finally, assist you in developing excellent, cutting-edge and future-proofed approaches to leadership. These will encourage our students to engage with transformative education – developing their understanding, skills and behaviours – thereby bringing about graduates capable of addressing the complex global challenges of today and the future.

**Stephanie Marshall**

# Part I
# A view from the top

# 1: Drivers and change

## OVERVIEW

As higher education (HE) globally is moving into an era of unprecedented change, we are facing uncharted challenges. As educators, we are constantly being told that the past is no longer a guide to the future. Sector-wide, individual higher education institutions (HEIs) are considering how best to determine their own futures. Making sense of this complexity and making the right choices requires agility and flexibility, alongside skillful leadership and management of organisational change. This chapter, therefore, seeks to explore current key drivers of change, and their impact at three levels:

- the global level;
- the government level (i.e. HE policy);
- the individual institution level, with a particular focus on leaders of teaching and learning in HE (i.e. responsible for both translating policy into practice, at the same time as offering their own distinctive approach to delivery).

How these challenges have been interpreted and 'made sense of' (Weick and Sutcliffe 2007) is crucial to the success of an HEI. Indeed, those leaders who have responded in a constructive and positive manner to the international, national and local (institutional) drivers of change have found it easier to engage their staff in the journey (Gibbs *et al*. 2009). This approach of embracing the changes is crucial to ensure that graduates are well equipped to accept and respond intelligently to the challenges of a vastly different future.

## GLOBAL PERSPECTIVE

Since the 1970s, higher education in developed countries has moved beyond an elite system to one that is more accessible and inclusive. It has expanded enormously, widening its offer with respect to the diversity of subjects offered at degree level and modes of study, and is being delivered by an ever-increasing range of providers. Access to HE, retention, progression and success through to employment are all key issues across the globe. Responses to such drivers have been an increase in **blended learning**, redesigning learning spaces (to include **virtual engagement**) and attempts to **measure learning** and demonstrate return on investment as the cost of HE increases faster than inflation. Ministerial targets for participation in HE across the globe have led to a significant growth in student numbers. Additionally, not only have the numbers of indigenous students increased, but also those from an international market. The growth in numbers of international students seeking undergraduate education outside their own country has been particularly significant and important over the past twenty years.

This chapter will demonstrate to readers that leadership in the global HE system should now be viewed not just as a delivering the greater good (Collini 2012) but also running a successful business providing high-quality graduates to the labour market across the modern world. Global competition between universities to attract international students is intensifying, as is the competition for high-flying staff as excellent researchers but also, now, as excellent teachers. Responding to these drivers, and leading HE at all levels (i.e. globally, nationally and locally), has never been more challenging.

Beyond the importance of international students to the financial health of the higher education sector, there are four recurrent issues within HE for nations wanting to ensure that their providers are offering students a world-class learning experience. Each requires insightful leadership, with each being considered in differing degrees in the case studies which follow:

1   **Curriculum development.** Curriculum has had to become more multi-faceted in terms of content and use of global case studies and examples. Integral to a future-proofed curriculum are employability, internationalisation, sustainable development, and equality and diversity. These developments, combined with the move to greater interdisciplinary study, are helping universities to produce graduates capable of tackling key global issues.

2   **Innovative Pedagogies**. Advances in technology, **digital literacy** and blended learning approaches, alongside more simulations and work-based opportunities, are essential to inspire and engage students. Additionally, pedagogies which involve students as co-producers of knowledge are more likely to assist universities to develop the research capacity required for the future, particularly in STEM (science, technology, engineering, maths) subjects.
3   **Student transitions.** With nations providing greater access opportunities, consideration of how best to ease the transition into HE via different pathways needs to be addressed. Ensuring retention and success for each and every student, to include either transition to post-graduate study, graduate employment or self-employment, has to be a priority. Diverse learners need lecturers who are prepared to deploy diverse approaches.
4   **Staff transitions.** Lecturers are more aware, with students from diverse backgrounds and cultures in their classrooms, of the challenges of taking an inclusive approach and making fewer assumptions about cultural norms and reference points. Today's HE teachers need to appreciate the different educational experiences that form the background of many of their learners, who may have started their education in different traditions. Increasingly nations are looking to determine appropriate threshold professional standards for those involved in teaching, and teaching at different levels (e.g. programme director, head of school).

Iannelli and Huang (2014) draw attention to a number of these recurrent issues and argue that universities often underestimate the challenges and costs of properly supporting diverse students new to their HE system. An exploration of supportive and properly costed approaches is included in the case studies which follow.

---

### Interrogating practice

1   How are the issues, as presented above, addressed in your institution?
2   Are there any particular areas where you believe you could do better? How?

Rolf Tarrach, former President of the University of Luxemburg and now President of the European Universities Association (EUA), identifies three key drivers of change in HE: firstly, knowledge now being ubiquitous; secondly, the increase in student participation (with the associated concern to meet diverse learning needs); and, finally, the need to prepare students for employment, irrespective of discipline. He additionally argues for greater interdisciplinarity to better prepare our graduates for the future.

## Case study 1.1: Today's challenges in teaching

### Rolf Tarrach, European Universities Association (EUA)

It is a time of profound change. During the first thirty years of my adult life the *Encyclopaedia Britannica* was a reference work which helped me to find relevant information, and for a couple of centuries that has been the case for many scholars. I have seldom used it in the last twenty years since most information can now be instantaneously found on the web. This is great but has also led to an enormous amount of ubiquitous, non-vetted information, which could be put to good use. Today, this is one of the main challenges of education and a driver of change in HEIs: to learn how to find the information one is looking for efficiently, to be able to judge its quality and to know how to deal with it, so that it becomes knowledge.

A second driver is the democratisation and inclusiveness of today's HE: never before has the percentage of secondary school leavers who go to university been so high. This has two consequences: (a) it is difficult to keep the old standards if one does not want to increase the failure rate, and (b) a degree is no longer a guarantee of finding an adequate job and in some countries any job. Part of the solution to these changes is personalised teaching and more suitable pedagogy.

The third driver is partially a consequence of the second: it is the mismatch between the discipline-spectrum of degrees offered by HEIs and the skills sought by the job market, if not globally certainly locally. Indeed, a considerable amount of teaching supposes most students will get a job in academia or blue-sky research, which evidence tells us is not the case. If this is not dealt with, mobility (i.e. migration) is often the only solution left for graduates. Well-selected adjunct staff providing a large part of the teaching is one of the responses to this challenge, in addition to appropriate changes to syllabii.

There is a further step to be taken if we want education to be gold- (or even platinum- !) starred: to learn how to turn knowledge into understanding, i.e. to be able to explain the causes of something, allowing us to guess and assess the consequences within a wider context. But this is nothing new; it was always like this, but it is a notion that continues to be little heeded. To tackle this we need to move away from *Fachidioten* (i.e. specialists, expert in their field, who only see a multi-faceted problem through the lens of their own discipline), to bring about the genuinely interdisciplinary teacher.

Now, having learnt how to retrieve information, how to turn it first into knowledge and finally into understanding, what do we need it for? For almost everything, but in particular for assessing and solving the problems we encounter in our personal and pro-fessional lives as well as those of mankind. And this also tells us how to teach: start with a real, simple problem, and then acquire the information and the knowledge you need to deal with it. You don't understand a problem until you have a rough blueprint of its solution, and you don't find the correct solution without under-standing it. Teaching has to help us to quickly find what we need.

For all this, undergraduate teaching is the most important; that is where the best teachers should be, since it is here that the poten-tial added value of good teaching is greatest.

---

Much of the vision and methodology proposed by Tarrach is in the European Commission Report (2013) which appeals for universities to focus on the preparation of graduates capable of addressing the global **wicked issues**. This can only be achieved by moving away from subject specialism to interdisciplinarity. Tarrach is arguing for an HE system which produces critical thinkers, problem solvers and those with an appetite for working across boundaries, generating new knowledge and understanding. To bring about such change requires visionary leadership, whereby the desired skills, behaviours and capa-bilities expected of graduates are modelled by the leadership. An institutional leader's key delivery mechanism for bringing about such change is the curriculum.

> **Interrogating practice**
>
> 1    How are your graduates prepared to tackle the world's 'wicked issues', viewing them through the lens of the different disciplines?
> 2    How well are your staff equipped to offer such disciplinary approaches? Could more be done to inform and support them?

Following on from Tarrach's plea for greater interdisciplinarity to prepare graduates for an unknown future, Sir Alan Langlands, in Case study 1.2, focuses on this delivery mechanism, highlighting the centrality of the curriculum to the learning outcomes of students. He outlines a rich and multi-layered curriculum, which has been a response to his commitment to widen participation, and prepare each and every graduate to lead fulfilled lives. Whilst recognising the need for continuity, he additionally implores leaders 'not to be afraid of change'.

## Case study 1.2: A view from the top

### Sir Alan Langlands, University of Leeds

I have held chief executive or equivalent posts for more than thirty-five years but, with a strong hinterland in healthcare, I still regard myself as a relative newcomer to HE. That said, I have developed my insights into 'student education' – the term we use at Leeds to replace 'teaching and learning' – under the watchful eyes of Vivien Jones (University of Leeds, Pro-Vice-Chancellor, Teaching and Learning), Heather Fry (**Higher Education Funding Council England**) and James Calderhead (Vice-Principal, University of Dundee).

All three have taught me the importance of increasing knowledge and opportunity in powerful combination. This means providing outstanding education and opportunities for all-round personal growth for both undergraduate and postgraduate students. In an increasingly competitive environment, this gives the best universities a fighting chance of attracting, exciting and retaining high-quality students from diverse backgrounds, equipping them to succeed in a competitive global employment market and to make a difference to society and the economy. All three also encouraged my instinctive commitment to widening participation – spotting talent early and boosting the aspirations, and attainment and achievement of young people from challenging backgrounds.

The Leeds case is a testament to the expertise, professionalism and determination of Vivien Jones. Our new curriculum underlines the importance of research-based learning and final-year projects, incorporates a commitment to ensuring that students are exposed to global and cultural insights, has a framework of ethics and responsibility and employability skills, and broadens student experience through a range of elective 'Discovery Themes', and our LeedsforLife programme which focuses on the co-curricular – study abroad, work placements, volunteering, enterprise and so much more.

All of this is underpinned by an enlightened approach to student engagement – in our case a sector-leading Partnership (yes it is a capital P) with the Leeds University Union and wider student body – and an integrated student education service in which academic and professional staff work hand in glove. Looking more widely, mobility of people and programmes, the imperative of interdisciplinary working and advances in digital learning are also driving curriculum development and putting a premium on training and development to support teaching excellence.

This book underpins the **Higher Education Academy's** development programme for aspiring or existing pro-vice-chancellors or vice-principals who hold the teaching, learning and student experience portfolio, in a wide range of universities. This is an important role which will affect the lives and life chances of successive generations of students under your watch.

In these circumstances, you can afford to take time to understand the context in which you are operating, plan carefully and adopt a tone of voice which ensures that your students, colleagues and partners know what you stand for and what you care about. There is then the hardy annual point about finding the right balance between continuity and change. To quote from Alvin Kernan's memoir *In Plato's Cave*, allow your ideas to be 'smoothed against the grindstone of accumulated knowledge from the past and the real, present needs of an effective educational system.' So recognise the importance of continuity but do not be afraid to change. Healthy universities must have a capacity for renewal and you are an essential part of this process.

---

Langland's identification of the curriculum as central to the shaping of graduates is an important one. How often is curriculum development – let alone 'overhaul' – put into the box labeled 'too difficult for now'? Building in the capacity for renewal is crucial at a time of rapid change. And it is essential if institutions are to prepare their graduates not just for further study or employment at the point of graduation, but future-proofing their prospects by embedding flexibility and agility into their approaches to work and lifelong learning.

This capacity for renewal is illustrated in the next case study. In celebrating the University of Glasgow's embarkation on a major estates project to develop a new **learning and teaching hub**, Provost Anton Muscatelli, reflects on the key drivers that led to the decision to significantly invest in such a project. Similar to the two previous case studies, widened access, advances in technology, employability and the need for greater interdisciplinarity are viewed as the key drivers. Muscatelli views these challenges with excitement. He stresses the centrality of teaching and learning (indeed, placing the learner at the centre) as key to any HE mission. This requires today's HEIs to offer a sophisticated offer of blended learning and teaching informed by research, supported by a collective community to deliver an excellent learning experience. His plea is for leaders to be agile in developing exciting new ventures, hence his enthusiasm about Glasgow's new learning space.

## Case study 1.3: Building a learning and teaching hub

### Anton Muscatelli, University of Glasgow

The University of Glasgow is about to embark on a major, unprecedented development of its campus: an investment of £750 million. Our first agreed commitment is to build a new learning and teaching hub. It's an unequivocal statement of the priority we give to teaching.

Teaching is the raison d'être of the university. The Hub is a fantastic opportunity, not just to deliver a new and vibrant space for our learning community, but provides a focus for our thinking on how we can better provide and deploy our human resources, and our physical and virtual infrastructure, to deliver learning across campus for the twenty-first century and beyond.

We approach this opportunity with confidence and excitement because we build on great foundations. We're fortunate in that learning and teaching has been valued in Scotland for centuries. From its founding principles, the University of Glasgow has embodied this ethos and I'm proud of our commitment to teaching down through the years, and the consistent evidence that it's something we do well. It's a commitment that remains undiminished and at the centre of successive university strategies.

But why is it important?

1 It sends a clear and unequivocal message across the academic community that teaching and learning is core, critical and co-equal to the value we place on research.
2 Our teaching must be research-informed and research-led. We want learning to be infused with the excitement of discovery, inviting our students to be co-pioneers at the frontiers of knowledge.
3 It must be accessible. Underpinning Scotland's long history of exceptional education provision has been its inclusivity. I am proud of Glasgow's heritage in this regard. Today, we continue in this tradition, widening the circle of opportunity, expanding access to HE for talented students whatever their background.
4 We must be innovative in the way we teach. It was Frances Hutcheson, Professor of Moral Philosophy at Glasgow in the 1730s, who was the first in Europe to teach in English and he packed his classes. Today, we too are investing in new methods and approaches to deliver learning and teaching. **MOOCs** and online learning have opened up new opportunities: we launched four online degree programmes in November 2015,

with others scheduled for 2016 and others again the year after. These developments combine, as did Frances Hutcheson's initiative, innovation with accessibility.

5  We must place the learner at the centre of teaching and learning. This is critical if we are to understand and meet their needs. Hence our commitment to blended learning and the opportunity this provides for an improved learning experience through greater flexibility, important for what is an increasingly diverse, multicultural and international student community.

6  If we are to achieve these aims, we have to build and foster a strong and supportive environment, not just for the learner, but for our staff, our academic and support teams, enabling us to work together as a creative, scholarly, collaborative community. We have to blend together to create and sustain a place that lives, and celebrates, the value and importance of learning.

7  We must be agile in our capacity to develop new and exciting programmes, feeding off the energy of our diverse and international learning community. This will become ever more pressing as we look to develop more cross-university, interdisciplinary programmes and essential if we are to address the key challenges of our day.

---

Once again, we find it is the capacity of the university leader to embrace the drivers of change, demonstrating agility and flexibility of approach in terms of addressing the various components contributing to excellent learner outcomes (e.g. curriculum learning spaces, supportive community), whilst being mindful of the institution's vision and mission that brings success.

## Interrogating practice

1  Both Langlands and Muscatelli refer to 'Partnership' with students. What does 'students as partners' mean in the context of your institution?

2  Are there any aspects of 'students as partners' you could use to better support your students? If so, what are these?

## SUMMARY

This chapter examined a range of drivers of change in the HE education sector, with global trends such as economic imperatives leading to widened access, content becoming ubiquitous, blended learning – to include the full range of technological innovations, and the need for graduates 'fit for the purposes of employment'. All three case studies – from Luxemburg, England and Scotland – illustrate how university leaders are embracing these drivers of change, interpreting them and responding in constructive and engaged ways. All three leaders demonstrate an uplifting vision which they are passionate about delivering. In all three cases, the 'capacity for renewal' referred to by Langlands, is a constant.

In summary, HE leaders need to be agile and flexible, combined with being optimistic and confident that they can provide an offer that is really distinctive, exciting, and worthwhile for each and every one of their students. Delivering the best possible learner outcomes and subsequent impacts (be it at the individual, national or global level) must be at the fore. It is the leader's role to make sense of, and keep up with the drivers of rapid change, and either reinvent or recalibrate the various components of teaching excellence accordingly.

## FURTHER READING

Collini, S. (2012) *What are universities for?* London: Penguin.

A useful revisitation of the history and underpinning philosophy of universities going back to Newman's (1852) idea of a university. Useful to read to remind ourselves of the distance travelled, since moving from an elite to a mass system of HE.

European Commission (2013) *Modernisation of higher education: Improving the quality of teaching and learning in Europe's higher education institutions.* Brussels.

A really comprehensive overview of current European practice – proposing a vision for teaching and learning in Europe in 2020, drawing on case studies of best practice across the European nations, proposing a series of recommendations to both drive up the status of teaching and learning, at the same time as promote excellent practice, thereby preparing our graduates for a rapidly changing world.

Rizvi, S., Donnelly, K. and Barber, M. (2013) *An avalanche is coming: HE and the revolution ahead*. London: IPPR. Available from http://www.ippr.org/publications/an-avalanche-is-coming-higher-education-and-the-revolution-ahead (accessed 8 July 2015).

A provocative read which suggest with the advances and disruptive forces in technology, major transformation of HE is required. The authors suggest an 'unbundling' of the different contributory factors in delivery models across a diverse system that will obviate the traditional university of the past.

## REFERENCES

Collini, S. (2012) *What are universities for?* London: Penguin.

European Commission (2013) *Modernisation of higher education: Improving the quality of teaching and learning in Europe's higher education institutions.* Brussels.

Gibbs, G., Knapper, C. and Piccinin, S. (2009) *Departmental leadership of teaching in research-intensive institutions*. London: Higher Education Academy and Leadership Foundation for Higher Education.

Iannelli, C. and Huang, J. (2014) 'Trends in participation and attainment of Chinese students in UK higher education', *Studies in Higher Education*, 39(5): 805–822.

Weick, K. and Sutcliffe, K. (2007) *Managing the unexpected: Resilient performance in an age of uncertainty*. 2nd edn. San Francisco: Wiley.

# 2: Government and sector-led initiatives

## OVERVIEW

This chapter explores the changing character of teaching and learning in universities across the globe, comparing the responses of governments to funding issues and the market, enhancing social capital, and bringing about a more just society. Since the 1970s, higher education (HE) in developed countries has moved beyond an elite system to one that is more accessible and inclusive. HE systems have expanded enormously and widened their offer with respect to (i) the diversity of subjects available at degree level, (ii) mode of study (part-time, full-time, online, etc.) and (iii) range of providers (both public and private). This trend is across the world.

Most governments have shown leadership and set targets for HE participation with the norm being 40 per cent. Over the past thirty or so years, there has been a major shift in the way in which HE has been perceived, with an ever greater emphasis on social and economic capital. Alongside this concern has been the introduction of benchmarking, or comparison, as evidenced in the range of global league tables and rankings.

At the time of writing, there has been a significantly greater focus on the leadership of teaching and learning (particularly the drive for teaching excellence) at the sector level, featuring on both political and institutional agendas. This can be linked to, for example:

- new and/or higher fees regimes
- graduate unemployment (particularly in developed countries)
- international competitiveness (fuelled by the rapid rise of HE in the Far East)
- the promotion of students as global citizens.

This worldwide phenomenon has made it even more important for governments to focus investment in areas with the potential to reap the most return, with human capital to support the knowledge and skills economy being an obvious focus. Public and private funders of HE, seeking to gain competitive advantage, have thus sought to promote quality in teaching (to include the higher level skills agenda) with the same commitment that they have invested previously in research. There is now, as never before, a consensus that both research and teaching are vital to global economic and social wellbeing, with the latter (teaching) potentially providing a pipeline to the former (research). And to meet this challenge requires a clear strategy and capable leadership.

This chapter suggests that the global HE system is now not viewed solely as a means of delivering a greater good, and a selective pathway for a minority, but instead a successful business which can provide high quality graduates for a global labour market. Like any successful business, executive teams put much effort into determining an appropriate corporate strategy that will not only assist them to deliver their vision but also generate a healthy margin for reinvestment. For leaders of the teaching portfolio, no longer is reinvestment solely in research kit, but now, more than ever before, into enhanced learning spaces (e.g. **learning hubs**) and a wealth of additional student support. Some of the unique approaches that different governments across the globe have promulgated and led are explored in the rest of this chapter.

## THE US

The HE system of the US is largely decentralised and consists of public universities, private universities, liberal arts colleges and community colleges. Hence 'leadership across the sector' poses unique challenges. In terms of regulations, independent accreditation organisations (primarily six) quality assure and sign off the quality of degrees that are offered. The US has long been held up as an example of a system committed to equal opportunity and social mobility, with both the UK and Australia looking to emulate key success factors in addressing an inclusive agenda. High tuition fees, the marketisation of HE and student debt led to the US government, via the **Spellings Commission (2005),** to ask questions about the 'deal' – i.e. what students were getting in return for their investment – which they wanted to be examined throughout the universities of the US. Examination of 'the deal' in terms of inputs and outputs including attempts to measure **learning gain** led to various universities seeking to make their mark in nationwide leadership. Two examples follow.

The first initiative explores the concept of student engagement. The University of Illinois **National Student Survey of Engagement (NSSE)** provides a litmus test of the extent to which higher education institutions (HEIs) engage their students in learning, and, which particular approaches were engaging (or disengaging them) most successfully (or unsuccessfully). This survey – used for benchmarking purposes by vice-presidents (VPs) – is now used across the US on a voluntary basis.

A second initiative explores the concept of learning gain. Increasingly, VPs with responsibility for teaching and learning in the US are required to ensure that students are able to see where their tuition fees go, via transparent, publishable data. Thus the notion of 'learning gain' – as an indicator of distance travelled and worth – has taken hold with a number of universities using the Collegiate Assessment Tool to undertake pre- and post-programme testing to determine the value added of their degree programmes. Once again, this is a voluntary initiative and will remain so unless individual university leaders are sufficiently incentivised to take part.

## AUSTRALIA

To raise the status of teaching in learning in Australia, the **Australian Learning and Teaching Council (ALTC)** was set up in 2003. With initial funding of $29.6 million (AUS) per annum from the national government, the ALTC's goal was to promote excellence in pedagogic practice. With a strapline of promoting 'enhanced learning for students through engaging the higher education sector in the identification, support and reward of outstanding and innovative teaching', five workstreams were identified, with three focusing on teacher excellence, and two focused on the development and maintenance of learning networks (i.e. disciplinary networks). Despite its strong leadership and success in driving up excellence in pedagogic practice, the ALTC saw at the beginning of 2011 its funding removed by the federal government as part of an overall trimming exercise to pay for flood recovery. A year later, the Australian government announced a new initiative, the **Office for Learning and Teaching (OLT)**, with funding of $50.1 million over three years. The remit for this group was to operate strategically to the benefit of the sector as a whole, as opposed to individual teacher excellence. The governance of this new body was thus to include more vice-chancellor/president and institutional leadership representation, in order to address the strategic needs of both HE generally and universities in particular. The OLT has reached the end of its three-year funding and the next strategic response is yet to be announced.

## EAST ASIA

East Asia is rapidly becoming the third major supplier of HE internationally, joining North America and Europe. Since 2000, in terms of absolute numbers enrolled in HE, East Asia has overtaken North America and Western Europe. As an overall percentage of the population, participation in HE in East Asia remains lower than in those regions, but the expansion has been rapid, centrally led and driven, and looks set to continue until at least 2020 (British Council 2012).

A key driver in this expansion of numbers in HE in East Asia has been economic, being viewed as providing high-level skills (technical, behavioural and thinking) as well as stimulating innovation and increasing research output. Several governments have made explicit commitments to HE by developing regional hubs with ambitious international student recruitment targets. Alongside this hub approach, adopted in some countries like Thailand, Singapore, Malaysia, China and South Korea, some countries have set clear targets to upskill the nation's workforce and benefit the local economy, for example:

1   South Korea initiated the **National Project Toward Building World Class Universities** in response to the concern about the small number of international students they were attracting. In the first instance, the project was designed to attract highly qualified professors and researchers to Korean universities, which, in turn, could attract more international collaboration and partnership working. Inward mobility of students to Korea has been a particular success at the University of Seoul.
2   In China, a huge programme of investment and expansion is underway (OBHE 2013).
3   Singapore, further to the government setting a target to increase its participation rate in HE to 40 per cent, sought to determine a differentiated set of pathways for post-secondary students. Beyond

this, the National University of Singapore (NUS) has pioneered and led new approaches to gain more international engagement such as:

- global education
- experimental entrepreneurship education
- strategic partnerships (e.g. with Yale).

Such government policies around the world, which have been strongly translated into practice by institutional leaders of teaching and learning, have assisted the drive to recruit better staff and students who, in turn, have been able to move on to shape the future either via postgraduate work or graduate jobs.

## THE EUROPEAN UNION

### *Europe*

In 2012–13, the European Commission conducted an exploration of the current state of teaching and learning across the European States.

To address global competition, certain European governments have invested in setting up 'hubs' to support the development and dissemination of thought leadership and best practice in HE, and to promote efficiencies with respect to raising their profile in teaching and learning and hence their ability to attract the brightest and the best. For example:

1   The UK government underwrote the setting up the **Higher Education Academy (HEA)** in 2004 to provide central support for institutional strategies for the enhancement of teaching and learning. The remit covered curriculum development, innovative pedagogies – to include **digital literacy**, student transitions – access, retention and staff transitions – with an overall aim to support the professionalisation of teaching staff. Concurrently in 2004, in the UK, the **Leadership Foundation for Higher Education (LF)** was set up with a view to strengthening the capacity of leadership, management and governance in HE to cope with a major agenda for change.
2   The Irish government set up a **National Forum for the Enhancement of Teaching and Learning** in 2012, with a similar mission to that of the HEA in the UK.

3   The German government integrated its **Excellence Initiative** – initially addressing the research agenda to extend to teaching and learning, with ten selected HEIs working on the **Charter for Good Teaching**, and a national investment of €20 billion until 2020. Like other European nations, Germany has been focused on growing their own researchers, with the consequent requirement to enhance teaching and learning.

The leadership approaches deployed by these three countries – i.e. the UK, Ireland and Germany – are considered in the case studies offered below.

## The UK

The LF was granted £10 million over five years in 2003 to raise both the status and practice of leadership, management and governance of HE. Its initial focus was on executive teams – believing that without the capabilities and role modelling at the top of the organisation, there was little hope of best practice being sustainable beneath this level. Twelve years on, the various leadership development programmes offered by the LF are considered rites of passage for staff progressing through the various rungs of HE leadership careers.

> **Case study 2.1: The Leadership Foundation for Higher Education – inspiring leadership across the HE sector**

**Ewart Wooldridge, CBE, Founding CEO of the Leadership Foundation for Higher Education**

This case study is effectively the headlines of my eleven years of intensive engagement with leaders at all levels in HE institutions – as chief executive of the Leadership Foundation and more recently as an LF Associate – an exhilarating journey of opening up possibilities for leadership development in relation to teaching and learning, and all other facets of university life.

The immediate issues that I encountered (having come from other sectors into HE) were:

- Achieving senior institutional leadership roles was not seen as a natural career aspiration for core academic staff – as it would be for core talent in most other sectors. Many vice-chancellors spoke as if they had got into institutional leadership roles 'by accident'!
- 'Management' was viewed as a pejorative term – something that others did *to* you; or – a little more positively – as a rotational head of department, you served your three-year 'sentence' to support other academic colleagues and then returned to your 'real' academic role.
- Key professional staff who invariably were vital to the success of the institution, faculty or department were designated as '*non*-academics' – a strangely negative term which defined them by what they did *not* do!

The leadership of teaching and learning proved an elusive concept, and developing leadership programmes in this area was not easy. Our early successes were in the area of preparing HE staff for *institutional* leadership, through growing the success of the Top Management Programme for senior team members, and other national programmes to equip staff for strategic and departmental leadership.

In the academic domain, we made faster progress in the area of *research* team leadership development, perhaps because it was associated more with financial and resource management issues as well as academic leadership.

In the teaching domain, the breakthrough came with the publication of research jointly commissioned by the LF and the HEA, led by Professor Graham Gibbs, on Departmental Leadership of Teaching in Research-Intensive Environments (2009). This provided solid evidence in a majority of the case studies that 'leadership was important, and in many cases pivotal' to teaching excellence – and it was interesting that these were research intensive universities. Subsequent developments have included the LF/HEA collaborative programme on Leading the Transformation of Learning and Teaching, and the programme Leading Teaching Teams. Much was also learnt from the collaborative LF/HEA programme the Change Academy: placing academic leadership in the context of managing change which was vital, as was shown in the Gibbs research.

What have I learnt from this journey? Firstly, building the case for leadership development in HE, particularly for teaching and learning, needs to be evidence-based. The pedagogy needs to be grounded and relevant, not just imported from another sector or from generic programmes at a business school. Secondly, context is critical. Since the introduction of a student fees system for much of the UK, it has become axiomatic to respond comprehensively to the needs and voice of students and this has led a sea change in leadership thinking. Thirdly, the sector still, however, has a remarkable capacity to resist (or chooses to misunderstand) the case for leadership, as illustrated by evidence of the Bolden and Gosling research (2012) on academic leadership, which showed many academics remaining in denial!

Finally, is it wise to split leadership development in HE into the separate silos of teaching, research, professional and institutional? Whilst we may have had to disaggregate the territory to establish the case in each area, in the current market-driven world we inhabit, high-quality HE is a holistic experience, underpinned by cross-cutting academic and professional practice, and supported by collaborative leadership learning in a *shared* academic and professional space, as illustrated so persuasively by Celia Whitchurch's (2009) research into professional and academic careers.

The HE leadership development journey is by no means accomplished yet, but we are well beyond basecamp in making the case that leadership really matters in HE as in every other sector of society.

## REFERENCES

Bolden, R., Gosling, J., O'Brien, A., Peters, K., Ryan, M. and Haslam, S.A. (2012) *Academic leadership: Changing conceptions, identities and experiences in UK higher education*. London: Leadership Foundation for Higher Education.

Gibbs, G., Knapper, C. and Piccinin, S. (2009) *Departmental leadership of teaching in research-intensive institutions*. London: Leadership Foundation for Higher Education and Higher Education Academy.

Whitchurch, C. (2009) 'Progressing professional careers in UK higher education', *Perspectives: Policy and Practice in Higher Education*, 13(1): 3–10.

The key underlying message of Wooldridge's case study, based on bringing about change across the UK HE sector, is about raising ambition at the same time as going with the grain. To do so required the development of an evidence base (through research and effective sector engagement) to convince sceptics, alongside grounding the leadership development in the context of the strategic focus of the particular portfolio, e.g. Teaching and Learning.

---

### Interrogating practice

1  What is your reaction to the statement, cited in Case study 2.1, that leadership is important, and in many cases pivotal, to teaching excellence?
2  What leadership approaches are you witnessing in terms of translating national policy into institutional practice?

---

The next example, from Ireland, illustrates another government-led approach which has made rapid progress and a strong return on the investment. Once again, the approach used is one that clearly 'went with the grain', at the same time as raising ambition and expectation.

## Case study 2.2: Ireland's National Forum for the Enhancement of Teaching and Learning in Higher Education – engendering a sector-wide change culture

**Terry Maguire (Director) and Sarah Moore (Chair), National Forum for the Enhancement of Teaching and Learning in Higher Education**

Ireland's National Forum was established by the Minister for Education in 2012. Officially an advisory body to the **Higher Education Authority**, its declared vision and purpose is to act as an agent of change in Irish HE with a strong focus on a sector-wide approach to enhancing teaching and learning.

The Forum consists of a small directorate and is academically led. Its board represents key expertise within and beyond

Ireland's higher education sector, and it is guided by a panel of international advisors who bring ideas, enhancement practice and knowledge from across the world.

Steered by strong policy imperatives at national (see for example, Ireland's National Strategy for Higher Education to 2030) and European levels (see for example, the EU high-level group reports on improving the quality of teaching and learning and on new modes of learning), the Forum works in active and collaborative partnership with all Irish HEIs (universities, institutes of technology and private colleges in Ireland) to:

- reinforce teaching and learning effectiveness and excellence as core to the mission of Irish higher education;
- promote and generate parity of esteem between teaching and research;
- assist and facilitate the development of innovation in teaching and learning;
- build digital capacity and to enhance teaching and learning in a world that is increasingly digital;
- develop Ireland's strengths in evidence-based scholarly teaching and learning enhancement;
- celebrate outstanding teaching based on a rigourously developed learning impact award process, with explicit focus on encouraging and empowering student input.

The National Forum aims to continuously achieve these goals through consultation and by recognising the sometimes very different needs and priorities associated with teaching and learning enhancement at individual, departmental/disciplinary and institutional levels.

From a leadership perspective, it can be convincingly argued that a national entity that focuses strongly on teaching and learning is extremely timely. In a world where HEIs are expected to pursue an increasingly wide variety of multiple goals and where they are serving a wider diversity of constituencies, the sectoral approach to the core business of teaching and learning that the National Forum is pursuing seems particularly apt.

In a context like this, the National Forum's focus, support and facilitation when it comes to enhancing teaching and learning – as a central core function – aims to operate as a strategic ally to leaders in HEIs whose work has arguably become profoundly more complex and political. In addition, at a time of continuing financial constraint, there are clear economies of scale to be derived from the National Forum's sector-wide enhancement work.

The Forum has been set up to foster, support and create national approaches that take the best of what we do, identify synergies, and enhance the practice of all our institutions. The focus on adding value has been a consistent priority, and at all times the board of the Forum asks: 'Is the Forum helping to achieve sectoral goals with and on behalf of higher education that would be difficult for institutions to achieve on their own?' To ensure the involvement and collaboration of institutional leaders and to evaluate the work that the National Forum carries out, this question remains vital.

For further details see the National Forum's website: www. teachingandlearning.ie

---

The question posed in Case study 2.2 is a central one for all governments investing in a sector-wide approach, i.e. will the initiative help to achieve sectoral goals with and on behalf of HE that would be difficult for institutions to achieve on their own? The National Forum for the Enhancement of Teaching and Learning in Higher Education identified core goals for the sector, and also looked to identify synergies, economies of scale and exemplars of best practice.

---

### Interrogating practice

1  What central government initiatives have you engaged with and led within your institution?
2  What evaluative measures have been used as indicators of success?
3  When was the impact of the investment (in terms of either money or time) realised?

---

The third case study comes from Germany, where a major central government programme, the 'Excellence Initiative', saw significant investment made in research result in German universities become truly global in terms of positioning, recruitment, and league table rankings.

Such was the success of this investment, alongside concern to recalibrate the position the status of teaching, that it was decided to undertake a similar centrally led exercise focused on teaching and learning.

## Case study 2.3: Teaching and learning in German higher education

**Christian Tauch, German Rektors' Council**

German universities are proud of the Humboldtian tradition of 'unity of research and teaching' which laid the foundations for the success of German higher education in the nineteenth century. But 'unity' by no means implied parity of esteem – for decades, if not centuries, it was understood among German university professors that academic laurels were to be earned exclusively through excellence in research, but not in teaching. The most successful researchers often offloaded their teaching obligations to their young assistants who, in turn, tried to get rid of this chore quickly as they climbed the career ladder.

The situation has always been different at the Fachhochschulen, or universities of applied sciences. This type of HEI was first set up in the 1970s and a strong focus on application-oriented teaching has been one of their key features from the start.

In the aftermath of the Bologna Declaration of 1999 and the shift towards a two-tier structure of study programmes, a new discussion started in many countries of the emerging European higher education area, including Germany. It centred on the shift from teaching to learning, which was increasingly considered a keystone of the European study reform. German higher education institutions were, in addition to the Bologna reforms, facing the challenge of a rapidly growing and increasingly diverse student body, which placed a heavy responsibility in the institutions and called for new approaches to teaching and learning. Since the German higher education system is organised in a highly federal and decentralised way, the new discussion on learning outcomes-based teaching and assessments was not steered or masterminded by any central agency but developed through numerous initiatives and in various contexts.

One of the first attempts to achieve more parity of esteem between research and teaching was the Ars legendi award, initiated jointly by the Stifterverband für die Deutsche Wissenschaft and the German Rectors' Conference in 2006: €50,000 is awarded annually to an individual in recognition of his or her outstanding achievements in teaching (e.g. the 2015 prize is dedicated to excellence in digital teaching and learning).[1]

The German Rectors' Conference has been supporting its member institutions in their study reform efforts through a number of subsequent projects since 2005, all funded by the Federal Ministry of Education and Research. The most recent one, under the name Nexus – Forming Transitions, Promoting Student Success focuses on optimising the initial phase of studies, promoting mobility during a course and facilitating the transition to employment. Selected groups of experts in the engineering, business and healthcare/medical fields work with the project to develop generic solutions.[2]

Another important driver for the teaching and learning discussion was a call for proposals under the heading 'Excellent teaching', organised by the Stifterverband and the sixteen German ministers in charge of HE in 2009. Six universities and four universities of applied sciences were selected for the quality of their teaching and learning concepts and shared the €10 million prize money.[3] The ten winners subsequently worked together to draft a Charter for Good Teaching, published in 2012.[4]

The biggest initiative in the field of good teaching and learning so far has been the Quality Pact for Teaching that the German Federal Government and the sixteen Länder (states) set up in 2011: in two rounds of funding about €2 billion have been allocated to 186 HEIs for the period from 2011 to 2020. The funding serves to improve study conditions in three main areas: to increase staffing at institutions of higher education, to qualify staff in the areas of teaching, mentoring and advisory services and to give fresh impetus to the further development of teaching quality and to the professionalisation of teaching.[5]

A lot still remains to be done to achieve true parity of esteem between research and teaching in German higher education, in particular in the universities, but it is also true that huge progress has been made in the last fifteen years. It remains to be seen how the dozens of promising initiatives set up under the Quality Pact for Teaching can be made sustainable after the end of the project funding. This will not be an easy task, given the debt break that has been decided by the German Federal and Länder governments in 2011 and that imposes strict limitations for extra funding. But the sense of responsibility for their students and graduates that German HEIs have developed over the past years and that led to better teaching, mentoring and counselling is unlikely to disappear again.

## NOTES

1  http://www.hrk.de/themen/lehre/arbeitsfelder/ars-legendi/
2  http://www.hrk.de/activities/bologna-process/#c3855
3  http://www.stifterverband.info/wissenschaft_und_hochschule/lehre/exzellenz_in_ der_lehre/index.html
4  http://www.stifterverband.info/wissenschaft_und_hochschule/lehre/charta_guter_ lehre/charta_guter_lehre.pdf
5  http://www.bmbf.de/en/15375.php

This case study illustrates a government taking seriously the status of teaching in HE as a core activity requiring investment to both highlight excellent teaching but also upskill its staff. All three have similar visions in that they aspire to bring about an enhanced teaching workforce, committed to supporting the transformation of learning for their students. All recognise that without such investment their societies and economies will not thrive. And, as with any initiative destined to succeed, it needs to be well led.

## SUMMARY

This chapter makes no attempt to consider the full breadth or detail of internationalisation of HE teaching and learning. Its purpose was to indicate something of the extent of government-led investment in HE teaching in a global context, and drawing attention to the impact that has started to be made. In the three case studies offered here, major government investment has led to different strategies to incentivise the leadership of teaching in HE at both the national and institutional level. In all three case studies, central initiatives have been exceptionally well led, with on-going evaluation and impact being an important requirement to ensure return on investment. We, as committed educationists, need to ensure that the spirit of these initiatives continues, with the transformed practice becoming embedded in day-to-day practice. Our future is at stake otherwise.

## FURTHER READING

Courtney, S. (2014) *Teaching excellence: A literature review.* York: Higher Education Academy.

This review of the international literature on national teaching excellence initiatives is a most interesting read in terms of approaches which are clearly culturally specific. The trend is impressive with some really creative and innovative government initiatives providing some useful ideas as the global agenda gains momentum.

European Commission (2013) *Modernisation of higher education: Improving the quality of teaching and learning in Europe's higher education institutions.* Brussels.

A really comprehensive overview of current European practice – proposing a vision for teaching and learning in Europe in 2020, drawing on case studies of best practice across the European nations, proposing a series of recommendations to both drive up the status of teaching and learning, at the same time as promote excellent practice, thereby preparing our graduates for a rapidly changing world.

Higher Education Authority (2011) *National Strategy for Higher Education to 2030.* Available from http://www.hea.ie/sites/default/files/national_strategy_for_higher_education_2030.pdf (accessed 15 August 2015).

## REFERENCES

British Council (2012) *Going Global 2012: Identifying the Trends and Drivers of International Education.* Bingley: Emerald Group Publishing.
OBHE (2013) *Borderless Report.* Available from www.obhe.ac.uk/news letters/borderlessreport (accessed 18 August 2015).
Spellings Commission (2005) *The future of higher education.* Washington: US Department of Education.

# 3: Governance and leadership

## OVERVIEW

A sound understanding of higher education (HE) governance, and the way in which leadership interfaces with the governance infrastructure, is essential for any executive leader. From working with a higher education institution's (HEI) board, right down to school or departmental committees, the executive leader is responsible (and accountable) for aligning resources with the proposed delivery mechanism. However, before even thinking about resources, it is important that the VP (Teaching and Learning) has not only the confidence of their line manager, but also the institution's board or council. The board will expect to be kept informed (and, indeed, consulted) regarding justification for firstly, the strategic vision for teaching and learning that is proposed; secondly, the strategic resource implications; and, finally, narrative around ongoing monitoring and evaluative data of the various instruments of accountability. In the chapter that follows, these aspects of governance will be covered in more detail through closer examination of three areas: what exactly is meant by 'governance'; why it is so important for a VP (Teaching and Learning) to attend to relationship management across the governance infrastructure (up, across, and down); and finally, looking through the lens of the chair of the board to provide some final insights.

## GOVERNANCE: WHAT IT IS, AND WHY IT IS IMPORTANT

Ask any member of staff in an HEI what they think 'governance' means, and the majority will give a noun such as the **board, council** or 'governors'. Few will appreciate that governance is a complex set of interrelationships, usually embodied in a committee structure with delegated responsibilities which provides checks and balances to the strategic decision-making process and resource allocation. 'Boards' (a generic term which will be used to include councils, governors, and courts) have a complex role in that they are in the business of providing public accountability. At the same time, the lay members bring expertise from their experiences gained from the wider, often corporate world. By and large, they will have had extensive experience of executive leadership, and thus have accompanying expertise which will help inform corporate decisions on finance, estates, human resource (HR) management and IT. They may need help, however, in understanding how universities actually work. The institution's student president also is a member of the board, and many HEIs more recently have appointed more than one representative of the student body. As a consequence, as well as looking at the overall corporate strategy, the board applies serious scrutiny to the sub-strategies such as research, teaching and learning, the student experience, IT, estates and HR. They scrutinize the overall impact of the strategy on the student experience, using ongoing survey data and **learning analytics**. In the UK, much guidance is provided to governors via the **Council of University Chairs (CUC)**. Over the past decade, the CUC has assisted the sector with a modernising agenda for governors, bring HE governance and accountability much more in line with the corporate world and, most importantly, the **Nolan Principles**. Their most recent guidance is referred to in the case study provided by Robin Middlehurst, which succinctly outlines this modernising agenda, which is very much about 'protecting the collective student interest'.

## Case study 3.1: Governance and leadership

### Robin Middlehurst, Kingston University and Higher Education Academy

Embodied in the concept and practice of UK universities lie significant public responsibilities. These include the power to assess students for the award of undergraduate and postgraduate degrees (often leading to a licence to practice); designing appropriate curricula for educating twenty-first-century professionals, entrepreneurs and citizens; sustaining academic freedom and upholding academic standards; and monitoring, developing and enhancing the quality of higher learning offered by universities. These leadership and stewardship responsibilities are exercised corporately and collectively by the university's governing body (council, board of governors or court), by the vice-chancellor or principal as chief academic officer, through shared governance arrangements with the senate, senatus or academic board and its sub-committees, and through developing a deep and pervasive quality culture throughout the academic and professional communities of the university. These responsibilities require serious focus and attention from those who occupy governance and leadership positions – at all levels – within the corporate, executive and collegial system.

Two new higher education codes of governance (see References) have been published that spell out the values, principles and expectations underpinning the conduct of governors and relationships with the executive, institutional staff, external stakeholders and partnership with students for all types of HE providers. The CUC Code outlines the Core Values of Higher Education Governance, building on the Nolan Principles of Public Life. These core values are directly related to learning, teaching and students' expectations and experience of higher education. Through adopting the Code, governing bodies are expected to commit to:

- autonomy as the best guarantee of quality and international reputation;
- academic freedom and high-quality research, scholarship and teaching;
- protecting the collective student interest through good governance;
- the publication of accurate and transparent information that is publicly accessible;
- a recognition that accountability for funding derived directly from stakeholders requires HEIs to be clear that they are in a contract with stakeholders who pay for their service and expect clarity about what is received;
- the achievement of equality of opportunity and diversity throughout the institution;

- the principle that HE should be available to all those who are able to benefit from it;
- full and transparent accountability for public funding.

Separate guidance offers practical advice to governors on how they can exercise their duties in relation to academic standards, quality and 'the student experience' (Middlehurst, 2011) in an increasingly dynamic and competitive marketplace for HE with a diversity of providers and provision offered domestically, internationally and increasingly online. Good governance and effective leadership lie at the heart of maintaining academic health and sustainability, delivering a high quality student experience, supporting and enhancing high quality and innovative teaching, ensuring student success and maintaining the UK's reputation for providing excellent HE.

## REFERENCES

Committee of Scottish Chairs (2013) *Scottish Code of Good Higher Education Governance*. Available from http://scottishuniversitygovernance. ac.uk/wp-content/upload/2013/07/Scottish-Code-of-Good-HE-Governance.pdf (accessed 14 August 2015).
Committee of University Chairs (2014) *The Higher Education Code of Governance*. Available from http://www.universitychairs.ac.uk/wp-content/uploads/2015/02/Code-Final.pdf (accessed 14 August 2015).
Middlehurst, R. (2011) *Getting to grips with academic standards, quality, and the student experience*. London: Leadership Foundation for Higher Education.

Core value 4 in Case study 3.1 refers to the 'publication of accurate and transparent information that is publicly accessible'. It is worth unpacking what exactly this means. VPs (Teaching and Learning) are often 'measured' by the extent that they are able to deliver year-on-year improvements in a range of areas – with core metrics often used for benchmarking purposes.

For example, since the early 1990s, all HEIs have had to provide greater accountability to their boards with respect to student numbers: recruitment, retention, degree success and, more recently, progress through to employment. Undoubtedly the **National Student Survey (NSS)**, introduced in 2004 by the Higher Education Funding Council for England (HEFCE) has been the biggest game changer in that it has required a heightened focus on the learner experience. The results of the NSS were rapidly converted into league tables, with HE providers seeking to come top of the ranking (or at least making significant year-on-year improvements) thereby gaining significant prestige. Mission groups undertake benchmarking with their peers: for example, aspiring to be placed top of the Russell Group of universities. Woe betide any VP who does not take sufficient account of the NSS results, let alone the accompanying league tables!

---

### Interrogating practice

1   What **key performance indicators (KPIs)** of teaching and learning do your governors (or equivalent) review to monitor accountability?

2   Are these the right KPIs? Or might there be others which are essential in terms of indicators that the institution places students at the centre?

---

The range of 'instruments of accountability', beyond the NSS and the other basic data as highlighted above that the board normally require VPs to report on, include: the Destination to Employment of Leavers in Higher Education (DELHE), degree results with associated demographics, transition through to postgraduate education, and, increasingly, an analysis of **differential attainment**. With all these **key performance indicators** to be achieved, how best might the VP engage staff to assist in their achievement? This is where relationships at all levels are absolutely crucial.

## GOVERNANCE RELATIONSHIPS: WORKING EFFECTIVELY WITH GOVERNORS OR TRUSTEES

When listening to VPs talking about their experiences of working with the Board, I was fascinating to hear how many had been exceptionally nervous about presenting to the them (which a number referred to as 'the great and the good'). They wished they had had some tips and techniques before making their first presentation, which in many instances was to put forward a strategic paper which required board approval for investment. Some of the tips and techniques that might help readers are given below, and illustrated in Case study 3.2, and offer an opportunity to reflect on your own situation.

Preparing for board meetings requires much choreography, including rehearsal, to ensure that beyond the preparation of papers and anticipation of questions, you are able to conduct yourself confidently, knowing which particular issues you are prepared to push back on, and which you would be satisfied to note, take away or reconsider. Ensure when you are doing the final preparation for the board meeting that you have not only done your homework but also gathered sufficient evidence to support your arguments and have the data to hand to answer questions. Undoubtedly your executive colleagues will help out where they can, but this is your portfolio and your executive colleagues, particularly your president (or vice-chancellor or principal), will expect you to perform well. It reflects poorly on the whole senior executive if you are not a solid and capable member of the team (see Chapter 6).

Present with confidence and remember that less is more as the majority of people on the Board are lay people – they don't want an academic treatise in response to a question. Listen very carefully to their questions too. The board will have confidence in you if you consider their questions carefully, are not defensive and answer as clearly as you can – even if it is to note that they have made an interesting point that is worth spending a bit more time pursuing. The chair will be a good ally if board members see that what you are suggesting will ensure the future success of the institution, by way of a realistic, time-bound and well-considered proposal, that clearly has been aired and signed off by the relevant committees within the institution (i.e. you have undertaken due diligence prior to taking the paper to the board).

## Case study 3.2: Maintaining governance relationships

### Alistair Sambell, Edinburgh Napier University

Just over three years ago I was appointed as vice-principal (Academic), responsible for teaching and learning, research and the academic portfolio across the university. Around eighteen months after my appointment, following a change of vice-chancellor, my role changed to a wider remit as sole vice-principal and deputy-vice-chancellor, retaining responsibility for the academic activity.

One of the things we prioritised following the new VC's appointment was the development of a new strategy for the university, and I had particular responsibility for developing the academic strategy. I wanted to increase the direct ownership of the strategy and remove some of the decision-making layers by simplifying the academic structure and aligning research more closely with teaching. A key element of the structure I inherited was research being focused within nine separate research institutes; however, my view was their performance was very mixed. The structure was also starting to be inhibiting rather than enabling, and was leading to a dislocation of activity in the university. We agreed we would look to realign and reintegrate the institutes within the overall academic management structure.

Once you undertake a project like this it becomes high profile and many people, with a number of vested interests, have an opinion. There are three important things to consider when working to gain governing body buy-in for such proposed change: firstly, be clear and consistent about the underlying drivers of what you are trying to achieve; secondly, lay careful foundations during the consultation period to engage key people; and finally, have a clear timeline of what is happening when.

The first part requires a clear set of high-level principles that articulate drivers and objectives. In our case, this centred on the critical role of both teaching and research within a university and the linkages between these activities. The need to improve performance, in a sustainable manner, would be essential to underpinning our future success. Making the case for change required linking the external context and business realities whilst also presenting clear benchmarked academic and financial performance indicators, trends and future external drivers. An understanding of real figures, based on current performance, was indispensable in setting the need for the changes behind the big academic strategy piece.

It is important, then, to have an open, clear consultation period. This is made up of both the formal consultation meetings and putting the time into having the informal conversations. It is critical to understand who has vested interests. Some of these people are going to be persuadable, others will be unpersuadable and will be adamant that what you are doing is the worst thing that has ever been conceived. You should not underestimate the informal networks that exist and which you may not know are a whole range of contacts that interact with the governing body. The more you can invest in making sure people involved get direct, clear information the more likely they are to buy in to the proposed change.

We set up an informal advisory board to assist with our consultation on structure changes; it included representatives from the governing body. This board was not part of the formal university governance structures but formed to help obtain buy-in and provide reassurance to the governing body that change was being appropriately managed. We also sought to engage the governing body by drawing on particular expertise they could offer on HR issues.

Another important part of the consultation period is finding some external voices saying the same things as you are. If you are trying to do something particularly difficult, credible independent externals who agree with what you are doing can be an important element of gaining the momentum for change.

Finally, it is important to have a clear timeline from the outset which communicates what is happening when so that consultation can be closed down and decisions made and implemented. Avoiding drift during major change is critical, as the fear of change is typically more unsettling than the change itself. So keep consultation moving forward and ensure regular reporting. We agreed a timeline for consultation, reporting back to the governing body regularly and with quick implementation following the agreed consultation period. We progressed the major changes as quickly as possible, dealing with detailed issues in due course, rather than trying to deal with every detail from the beginning. When you are making major change at a high structural level then there are lots of knock on consequences, but establishing the principle of that change and getting on with it minimises the risk of smaller issues or lower-level details growing arms and legs before you start.

> ### Interrogating practice
>
> 1 Consider the background of the different members of your Board. Who will be the immediate supporters of your proposal? Who might be the blockers? And who will want to raise shrewd financial or political questions?
> 2 Undertake a mapping exercise of Board members, and make the effort to request some time with those who will help you drill down into areas such as finance, and offer you feedback. It will be time well spent. Similarly, contact those you fear might be blockers (e.g. colleagues who say 'the last VP tried that and it did not work . . .') to ascertain what it is that they fear might go wrong. All these conversations could offer you some sound advice as to areas where you need to gather more data.

What does due diligence with the rest of the governance infrastructure look like? When considering a paper for the board, it is best to look at the date when one has to present (e.g. Sambell's 'timeline'), and work backwards from that date to determine a framework for both pitching a visionary idea, gaining feedback, undertaking evidence collection and working this vision up into a business case. Relationships with those leading the key committees or groups across the institution will be vital to securing ownership of the proposal and determining how to get others engaged in putting the effort and commitment into bringing about the proposed change. A useful example is provided in Case study 3.3, which outlines how one pro-vice-chancellor (Learning and Teaching) worked with his board to improve NSS scores via a five-year strategy, which involved significant strategic investment. This did not happen without constructive, positive and determined commitment at all levels of the university.

## LOOKING THROUGH THE LENS OF THE CHAIR

A sound working relationship with your board is essential to garner confidence that the vision and strategy for teaching, learning and the student experience have been carefully worked up as a result of:

1 an engaged and robust visioning exercise, led by the VP;
2 a gap analysis of the distance to be travelled to achieve the vision;
3 option generation (which will include global environmental scanning alongside resource implications of the different strategies) and option appraisal and recommendations;
4 pulling together the final corporate teaching and learning strategy which will include sensible KPIs that can be cascaded across the governance infrastructure, i.e. faculty boards, school boards, etc.

Geoff Dawson, Chair of Sheffield Hallam University at the time of writing, and Chair of the CUC, provides a useful insight into both his role, and the board's concern that one particular aspect of the university's strategy needed to be heightened and addressed : the NSS results. The board requested that the PVC (Teaching and Learning) improved NSS scores via a five-year strategy, which the PVC suggested would involve significant strategic investment. The PVC (Teaching and Learning) knew that his ultimate credibility with his staff was dependent on him negotiating support from the board for allocation of the necessary resources, which, it was suggested, were necessary if all concerned – board and the university – were serious about raising their NSS scores by ten points over five years. A focus on this particular instrument of accountability by the board has been replicated across the UK. Case study 3.3 offers a particularly useful insight into the way in which the board continued to interact with the VP (Teaching and Learning) – which was to 'continually encourage, provide challenge and monitor progress' – to achieve the vision for the student experience that was, and has been, so crucial to the university's success.

> ## Case study 3.3: A *very* personal 'view from the top' – the importance of teaching and learning in HEIs

### Geoff Dawson, Sheffield Hallam University

The landscape in UK higher education has changed dramatically in recent years. We have seen major changes in research funding policies, the introduction of a primarily student funded system for teaching, the opening-up of the sector to encourage new providers and the progressive liberalisation of student numbers and removal of limits on them. Added to that have been the changes to visa policies within an increasingly global higher education sector, and the disruptive effects of the internet and associated technology, and it is hardly surprising that there are some concerns as to just what the future holds for UK HE. The potential outcomes of these changes for the sector are perhaps more unclear than at any time since **Dearing** (1997) (National Committee of Inquiry into Higher Education).

One thing is clear, however, and about which there should be no uncertainty: central to the continued success of our sector will be the quality of teaching and the learning experience that our student body receives. With the empowerment of students to have much greater choice and much greater information about where to spend their money within HE, increasing the quality of the educational experience of students is not a 'nice to have', it is absolutely essential for all HEIs irrespective of their type or indeed standing.

The governing body (or its equivalent) has a key role to play in this. The balance of their decisions around the choices between additional expenditure on estates, technology (including IT infrastructure and applications) and staff are amongst the hardest decisions to get right. But they will be central to any attempt to increase teaching quality, and hence the key student satisfaction measures in the NSS.

The governing body must also provide a supportive yet challenging environment, within which the executive can carry out their plans to improve the student learning experience, ensure that the necessary investment funding is made available, and continually encourage, provide challenge and monitor progress in this. Innovative plans to increase recognition and reward, additional qualifications and certification, and enhanced promotion prospects for teaching staff should also be encouraged and supported. Similarly, measured steps to increase the use of technology in the teaching and learning environment, along with the provision of an up-to-date flexible estate with facilities that encourage modern learning experiences, are all key to the institution's success. But these activities nearly all require additional funds; these funds have to be made available.

And it is no use expecting things to improve overnight, they will not! This is a long term process of **culture change** to embed the reality of 'Students at the Heart of the System' within an HEI, and to demonstrate an unshakeable commitment to the improvement of teaching quality. So patience is another pre-requisite for success here, along with focus, and just the sheer determination to stick with it.

But it can bring real success. My own institution, having had a clear focus in this area over the last five years, has seen a ten-point improvement in its overall NSS score; we now enjoy our highest league table position ever, and we are amongst the most popular HEIs in the country in terms of applications from students who want to study with us. We cannot rest upon our laurels, but we seem to have made a great start!

## REFERENCE

Dearing, R. (1997) *Higher education in the learning society*. The Report of the National Committee of Inquiry into Higher Education (The Dearing Report). Available from http://www.leeds.ac.uk/educol/ncihe (accessed 14 August 2015).

## SUMMARY

This chapter considered what constitutes good governance from three different viewpoints: from an 'expert', an executive member preparing papers and presentations to gain board support, and a chair of governors. A central message of all three was the importance of ensuring good working relationships between all key players at board meetings – senior executive members, board members and the chair, maintaining an informed dialogue at informal and formal levels. Good relationships are vitally important.

Once you have additionally undertaken the analysis suggested in the two interrogating practice sections, you should have a good sense of the context for taking your strategy forward. In the UK, a key challenge ahead, which VPs (Teaching and Learning) are going to have to navigate, is the introduction of the new quality assurance arrangements, alongside, for England, a **Teaching Excellence**

**Framework (TEF)**. At the time of writing, initial discussions on the policy framework are underway, with the only 'known' being that the raising of student fees will be dependent on the successful introduction and delivery of 'quality teaching'. It is proposed that governing bodies have a significant role in assuring and validating these processes. Thus, discussions at an earlier rather than later stage will be essential.

In conclusion, governance – as with all types of leadership – is a contact sport. If you are not prepared to spend time with various key stakeholders, you will find it much more difficult to deliver results. This leads us on to the next chapter, which explores a different form of leadership, that of academic leadership.

## FURTHER READING

Greatbatch, D. (2014) *Governance in a changing environment: A literature review*. London: Leadership Foundation for Higher Education.

Alongside providing a review of the literature, focusing on the changing environment of governance, the review includes extracts from institutional effectiveness reviews, which can provide the reader with some useful pause for consideration.

*Getting to grips guides for governors*. Leadership Foundation for Higher Education. Available from https://www.lfhe.ac.uk/en/research-resources/publications/getting-to-grips.cfm (accessed 14 August 2015).

These guides – on the full range of core functions of an HEI, e.g. human resources, IT, estates – are invaluable for any reader wanting to gain an overview of the component parts of a university, considering how they fit together, and what good governance in the context of each is considered to be.

Shattock, M. (ed.) (2014) *International trends in university governance: Autonomy, self-governance and the distribution of authority*. London: Routledge.

For those whose appetite has been really whet with respect to the role of governance in HE, this volume of edited works is really useful for gaining an overview with respect to both the modernising trends alongside seismic shifts in HE, and how governance globally has had to change to accommodate these changes. Drawing on examples from a range of first world countries, such challenges as cross-border partnerships and collaborative research projects are explored.

# 4: Academic leadership

## OVERVIEW

> The [current challenge is around] ... leadership, charged with the challenges of developing the ... future and of building faculty vitality. As we move into the new millennium, we face a time of major change ... changing student clientele, disintegrating college curricula, growing technological changes, and shifting attitudes and practices of faculty represent some of the many forces currently shaping higher education ... Anticipating your changing environments, developing a future-orientated statement of ... mission, and providing leadership to unify ... activity towards a 'planned' future is the mark of effective leaders ... The time of 'amateur administration' where professors temporarily step into the administrative role ... has lost its effectiveness. The call is for academic leadership.
>
> (Gmelch and Miskin 1993: 1–2)

This statement, written over twenty years ago, still holds good today. Since Gmelch and Miskins's plea to articulate more accurately what the role of academic leadership entailed, and, indeed, provide development and training for such a role, much work has been undertaken. Prefacing the current chapter with this quotation serves as an important reminder to the reader that leadership does not take place in a vacuum – it has to be context-specific to enable the desired mission of the organization to be achieved. The interplay of external and internal drivers, the institutional mission and strategy, and the availability of resources (in short, everything covered in Chapter 8) are all essential to nuancing the academic leadership style required to be an effective and successful vice-president (VP).

Let's first examine how leadership of higher education (HE) might differ from leadership of business and enterprise, or, indeed, other public services such as schools. For some people, academic leadership is equated with collegiality, and a spirit of autonomy and self-determination. For others, the definition of 'academic leadership' continues to be contested. From the late 1980s, calls for greater accountability and transparency in the use of public funds led to calls for the professionalisation of leadership, management and governance practice in HE. Subsequently, a number of researchers (e.g. Gmelch 1993; Middlehurst 1993; Ramsden 1998) and leadership development specialists began to articulate a distinctive framework for conceptualising academic leadership and, indeed, emphasising its importance.

To assist our thinking, this chapter commences with a section providing an overview of perspectives on academic leadership. The second and third sections examine academic leadership in practice, from firstly, the perspectives of a VP and then secondly, a vice-chancellor. By the end of the chapter, readers should have a sense of the nuanced approach to leadership that academic leadership offers. It is through understanding and practising this nuancing that leaders will obtain the followership of groups and individuals, many of whom have exceptional talent, creativity and are global leaders in their own right.

## ACADEMIC LEADERSHIP: AN OVERVIEW OF PERSPECTIVES

If readers were hoping for a succinct one-sentence definition of academic leadership, then they will be disappointed. Various researchers over the last few decades have considered a range of definitions, typologies and frameworks, and it is worth a quick canter through these as each views academic leadership from different perspectives.

The continuing research of Gmelch (2013) has focused on 'transitions to leadership' and what the term means for academics moving forward in their careers. He looks particularly at the various personal transitions that will have to be taken to be successful (e.g. from operating as an individual to being the leader of a collective entity). His most recent study, with Buller (Gmelch and Buller 2015) draws on the 7S model (Peters and Waterman 1982) – strategy, structure, systems, staff, skills, style and shared values – to determine a practical approach to academic leadership development, which they see as core to delivering an institution's mission and strategy.

In contrast, examining Ramsden's (1998) 'domains of academic leadership', offers a useful four quadrant framework for conceptualising the role:

- academic leadership
- academic people
- academic management
- academic work.

This framework is highly context dependent, which obviously will vary according to the nature of the higher education institution. For those working in VP positions, much of the role and the way it is executed will derive from the distinctive institutional missions, corporate strategies, and the teaching and learning strategies which VPs inherit or will be required to develop and deliver. The four domains, as put forward by Ramsden, are predicated on an orginisation's conceptual framework being clearly understood.

Middlehurst (1993) considers the similarities and differences between generic leadership and academic leadership, exploring the behaviours required. Alongside some key generic behaviours, she emphasises that for an individual's leadership capabilities to be effective, they will need to be honed and nuanced according to institutional requirements. Harris *et al.* (2004) move beyond Middlehurst's model, exploring such honing and nuancing, providing a useful framework for effective leadership behaviour which resonates well with the findings of the survey of VPs undertaken for this book. This framework of capabilities and behaviours includes:

- an ethical approach whereby people are treated with respect
- effective communication
- developing a shared vision – particularly in connection with the development of teaching programmes and curricula – in conjunction with others
- networking
- empowering academic staff.

All highlight the need for academic leaders to be role models for others. They also emphasise the need for shared values (albeit not always explicitly mentioned), which brings us back to Gmelch and Miskin's (1993) overt reference to the importance and centrality of values.

For the purposes of this book, I shall define academic leadership as 'leaders leading academic endeavour', specifically those tasked with leading the development and delivery of teaching and learning. Furthermore, I would concur with Gmelch and Miskin (1993) that core values are essential to gaining engagement from all staff, and are demonstrated through 'walking the talk'.

---

### Interrogating practice

1   How do you define academic leadership?
2   Is academic leadership any different to corporate leadership? If so, how?
3   How does academic leadership present itself in your institution?

---

Over ten years ago I suggested that a key capability of any academic leader was 'sense making'. Sense making is derived from navigating the complex and turbulent external environment, translating this into internal policy and practice (Marshall 2007). Such an approach requires both agility and flexibility on the part of the leader, who needs to continue to focus on core academic business and its effective delivery. The trick is how to provide a conducive environment and relevant preconditions which facilitate the delivery of excellent teaching and research, whilst responding to the turbulence of the ever changing external landscape. With hindsight, I was presaging the testing of a new, more appropriate approach for academic leaders: structured improvisation. This approach is presented in Case study 4.1 below.

---

## Case study 4.1: A new approach to academic leadership – the case for structured improvisation

### Stephanie Marshall, Higher Education Academy

On reflecting where the sector is in terms of their thinking about academic leadership, it is clear that we need a model which is both agile and flexible, equipping leaders of institutions to operate effectively in a more fluid and rapidly changing environment.

A new approach will assist leaders to determine their own futures. Almost a decade ago now, when I was working at the Leadership Foundation for Higher Education (LF), I noted that there were three major changes that were impacting on the role of academic leadership. Firstly, we saw the advent of the knowledge economy, which required leaders to become adept at accessing expert knowledge, rather than holding it themselves. Secondly, there was the drive for talent, and talent management, with the key question: 'once you have grown or recruited the talent, how do you retain these employees?' And thirdly, there was concern for distinctiveness in brand and identity, as HE had become a highly competitive market. I posited the view that academic leadership was required in all key strategic roles, and therefore should be viewed as a more fluid process, supporting leadership and management in the ever-changing external landscape. In sounding out senior staff within higher education institutions (HEIs), I built up an approach which went on to underpin and inform a series of workshops.

This approach requires the academic leader to be absolutely clear about the end goal (i.e. success measures to be delivered in a fixed period of time). The task, then, for academic leaders is to draw out the expertise of a range of staff (if not all) to ensure this end goal is delivered to time; that is to say, engage 'followership'. The conundrum that many an academic leader faces is that a number of staff do not necessarily categorise themselves as 'followers'. Indeed, many are leaders in their own fields, and resist the notion of being 'led' or 'managed'. So, how might a leader gain the requisite followership?

At first, I equated this specific leadership challenge to the role of the conductor of an orchestra, with the following model:

As I trialled this notion in a few leadership development workshops, and, influenced by discussions with various individuals most particularly Gareth Jones (Goffee and Jones 2009), I came to view academic leadership as more akin to that of a jazz leader, i.e. much more attuned to individual expertise and able to flex and flow in response to the personal performance of individual players, i.e. structured improvisation. In universities, I observed that the 'best' academic leaders knew just how to attract and retain the brightest and the best, whilst noting that these talented bright individuals are also often the most difficult to lead, let alone manage. I thus looked to the work of a number of leaders in creative

Table 4.1 Two leadership approaches

| University or college | Orchestra or jazz |
|---|---|
| **Mission** To be 'best in class' | **Mission** To be 'best in class' |
| **Strategy** (Teaching & Learning) Interpret a range of policies to demonstrate a distinctive approach, e.g. Education for Sustainable Development, and where possible, new and innovative approaches. | **Strategy** Interpret a piece of work to illustrate the excellence of the collective players and individuals where appropriate. |
| **Resourcing** Seeking out, recruiting and developing talent to ensure that there are the right number of staff to deliver the core workstream areas, with distributed leadership and management. | **Resourcing** Seeking out, recruiting and developing talent to ensure the requisite number of players in the different sections, with leadership provided by section heads/first chairs. |
| **Performance measures** Key performance measures derived from the corporate strategy; all achieved or exceeded. | **Performance measures** Precision and excellence in delivery. Goal – performances measures achieved or exceeded. |
| **External marketing** League table positioning in large part derived from achievement of key performance measures, i.e. outcomes. | **External marketing** Positioning derived from external judgements re: the excellence and precision of delivery (e.g. enjoying the process) and overall conducting that achieves success and the 'wow' factor. |

jazz, to reflect on how they engaged and retained their mavericks. Rather than precision in anything other than technical skill, what I witnessed was a fluidity that the leader skilfully facilitated to achieve the desired goal (i.e. exceptional performance within a prescribed timeframe). For example, I looked at the evolution of Dave Brubeck's performance of 'Take Five' over a series of decades. In his early 1960s performances, his leadership was a steady, consistent, engaging piano backbeat. A few decades later, the confidence and ease with which Brubeck led these later performances illustrated a move to shared leadership. The passing of the 'leadership' from member to member was most noticeable. Observing these performances, one cannot help but notice the absolute trust between all the players. Brubeck's role had evolved to one which encouraged the 'stars' literally to step up when the opportunity was right, and then step back to allow others to contribute and become stars in their own right, at appropriate times. Throughout, Brubeck maintained the backbeat, so as to achieve an exceptional collaborative outcome. There was clearly an overall structure, an ebb and flow which can be likened to an organic academic strategy: two of the core skills of a jazz ensemble being *listening* to the other members of the ensemble and *engaging* with the listener. The term 'structured improvisation' best sums up both the jazz process and, I would argue, effective academic leadership.

---

### Interrogating practice

1  To what extent do you see academic leadership as 'structured improvisation'? When and where is such an approach used to best effect?
2  What other academic leadership frameworks have informed your practice? How has your practice evolved over time?

---

Highly effective leadership skills, as demonstrated by the jazz leader drawing out the different and unique contributions that various participants can make, are the best means of gaining full engagement. In essence, the academic leader needs to encourage staff to view themselves as volunteers in a most worthwhile collective endeavour. The following case study offers a most useful reflection on a flexible yet structured academic leadership approach, focusing on the end goal, required to get things done.

### Case study 4.2: Academic leadership in practice – a pro-vice-chancellor's perspective

#### Pauline E. Kneale, Plymouth University

Essentially, it's all about the people, (and a huge bucket of common sense).

Consideration of these wise words from Drucker, Biggs and Tang, McCaffrey, Barnett and many others are great for tactics, policies and approaches, but it's worth remembering every senior leader in HE brings with them the legacy of their discipline's culture and research approaches. Is your medical colleague a surgeon or a physician? Hydrologists seek to define 'the worst possible' flood, drought or water quality disaster, plan to manage this event, understand that's unaffordable and design what can be afforded. In this job the worst possible *Daily Mail* headline comes to mind. Trying to think through potential implications and mitigating potential difficulties is an important part of the role.

In flood management there is rarely enough information in the right timeframe to make an accurate forecast. In HE, even where there is plenty of corporate information, your heads of school, admissions tutors and others are likely to tell you it's wrong, out of date, inappropriately collected or any other excuse that comes to mind. Be comfortable in taking decisions with limited information, while remembering that, as with any first-year essay presented without evidence, the proposal will be challenged by esteemed colleagues reluctant to accept any change. Happily colleagues 'who get it' will get involved and role model the new process.

My favourite moment in any change proposal comes when colleagues are only prepared to be interested in an initiative if it is ground-breaking, enterprising and world-leading, but not prepared to implement it unless there is categorical evidence it is working elsewhere. This may politely be referred to as coping with ambiguity; there are less flattering descriptions.

Flexibility is crucial in pursuing a constant drive for enhancement in learning and the student experience. There are so many different elements to the agenda, and different schools and disciplines are in very different stages of development. Across a complex organisation part of the trick is working out and agreeing what needs to be done, while accepting that how it is done will vary. Keeping track of and encouraging 'go-slow' implementers is key.

Having acquired the learning and teaching portfolio, limited funds, few direct reports and a set of over 100 **regulatory frameworks** from the **QAA**, professional bodies, funding councils and others, most of which the average academic will not wish to be aware of, what do you do? Building networks to understand the institution, and providing informal and formal platforms to share ideas and establish groups to 'get stuff done' is essential. Crucial to success is meeting regularly with the faculty associate/pro-deans (Teaching and Learning), the quality team, the educational developers, the technology enhanced learning and other service leaders, including careers learning development and the registrar's office, especially those dealing with examinations, complaints and appeals. Establishing forums where large groups can discuss new initiatives, plan new policy and strategy and share experiences has been crucial.

Get outside your institution to identify regional, national and international developments presented for example at international HE learning and student experience conferences (**HERDSA, HEA, HETL, ISSOTL, SEDA, SOTL, SRHE**). What are the new initiatives, who is making effective changes, who should you be inviting to campus to talk to your staff?

Some questions to prompt thinking:

- What is the competition doing better?
- Why do some disciplines do better across-the-board, in particular **National Student Survey (NSS)** questions?
- How do you know what is really good teaching?
- What are the most exciting and effective learning experiences (seminars, workshops, practicals, etc.) on campus? How are these shared?
- What will be the exciting, challenging and effective learning activities in five years' time in your discipline?

At this level of seniority you cannot fix issues in the way you used to. You need to provide people with the space and confidence to do the fixing for the organisation , that is to say, its students. The trick is to keep people on the same agenda so that the fixes are aligned to regulatory requirements and an excellent student experience is delivered. Even so, *'He did what?'* may become your new mantra, because no matter how well organised and disseminated the strategy, policy, regulations and agreed process, people get off message.

In the longer term, universities will have to change with technology and new ways of learning. The next twenty years will be different, and the past will not necessarily be a good guide to the future. If nothing else, read Nedelescu (2013) and start the discussion.

## REFERENCES

Harris, J., Martin, B. and Agnew, W. (2004) 'The characteristics, behaviours, and training of effective educational/leadership chairs' in Thompson, D.C. and Crampton, F.E. (eds.) *The changing face(s) of educational leadership: UCEA at the crossroads*. Kansas City, Missouri.
Nedelescu, L. 'Why higher education requires a new underlying philosophy' at http://www.druckerforum.org/blog/?p=502

---

### Interrogating practice

1  Case study 4.2 refers to providing 'people with the space and confidence' to work on institutional priorities. How might such an approach translate to your context?
2  The case study also refers to 'the trick is to keep people on the same agenda'. How do you keep the focus on your agenda? Where might 'structured improvisation' come into this?

---

Finally, in Case study 4.3 we have a very different approach, driven by the vice-chancellor working closely with the PVC (Teaching and Learning) and all those involved in strategy development and delivery. In this case, the vice-chancellor (VC) sees himself very much as the central academic leader, distributing leadership throughout the university.

## ACADEMIC LEADERSHIP IN PRACTICE: A VICE-CHANCELLOR'S PERSPECTIVE

In the following case study, the vice-chancellor of the University of Ulster promotes academic leadership of teaching and learning as a collective endeavour, involving everyone – from council members through to those working in front-line delivery. Sir Richard Barnett (recently retired) offers a view of academic leadership which starts from the premise that the teaching and learning strategy, which has to be led from the top, i.e. the vice-chancellor, is the vehicle which unites everyone in the institution in the collective mission. Through engaging everyone in strategy development, delivery is achieved through 'distributed academic leadership'.

## Case study 4.3: Academic leadership in practice – a vice-chancellor's perspective

### Sir Richard Barnett, University of Ulster

This piece reflects on the role that a VC plays in academic leadership and the teaching and learning activities of a university. Most importantly, such activities must not only be important to the VC, but they must also be seen to be important to her/him. Whilst there will almost certainly be a pro-vice-chancellor (PVC) with responsibility for teaching and learning (and, increasingly, the student experience), leadership must be shared between the VC and the PVC. Together they must also ensure that leadership is distributed throughout the institution and that there is wide ownership of the initiatives. Leadership and ownership must include the **council** (governing body), senate (academic board), staff, students and partners such as professional bodies. A balance must also be struck between central (institution-wide) initiatives and complementary local (school level) initiatives. Contributions to teaching and learning must be reflected in the institution's reward and recognition policies.

This is a demanding agenda and over a period of ten years as a VC I have not always got it right. And some of what I have to say reflects lessons learned.

So what are some of the principal means by which this desired outcome is achieved?

It all begins with the development of the teaching and learning strategy. It is a mistake for a small group led by the PVC to develop a strategy and then to put it out for consultation. Instead consultation must start much earlier. A useful starting point is for a horizon-scanning and issues paper to be put together and for this to be discussed widely. In this context, I have found a single-issue joint meeting of council and senate to be useful. There will also be discussion through the usual formal structures – faculty and school boards, etc. But a series of 'town hall' meetings is also useful, to which all staff are invited. The VC should attend some of these **town hall meetings**, not as chair or principal speaker, but as listener. Discussions should also take place with a sample of key external stakeholders, such as **professional bodies**.

Further consultation will follow the subsequent development of the strategy. This extended process of developing the strategy serves to extend ownership of the strategy.

In terms of content the strategy must aim to achieve the all-important balance between institution-wide and school-specific initiatives. Staff and students take pride in the performance of their subject, especially when they have been involved in the development of the overall strategy and have local ownership of aspects of it. A subject team's involvement in the delivery of a strategy must never be in the form of compliance with initiatives developed elsewhere or imposed 'from above'. This leads to the danger of the subject team's involvement being in the form of the disastrous 'tick box' approach.

If teaching and learning is important – which it is for every institution – it must be reflected in the recognition and reward systems of the institution. In particular promotion – up to the level of professor – must be available for those whose principal contributions are in this area. And such promotions must be publicised widely. When such routes to promotion are introduced staff remain sceptical about whether the university is serious, and teaching and learning really does have parity of esteem with research.

Finally, it must be recognised that leading in teaching and learning is much more challenging than is leading in research. It is much easier for the individual to set their own agenda in research where individual- and institution-level aspirations tend to be closely aligned. By contrast, in teaching and learning individuals are making a contribution to a collective endeavour. A collective endeavour which must be owned by everyone. That is the tough agenda for leading in teaching and learning.

> **Interrogating practice**
>
> 1 How much does the approach used in your institution res-
>   onate with Case study 4.3?
> 2 Are there any approaches to gaining academic staff buy
>   in which you have picked up as a result of the three case
>   studies offered in this chapter? If so, how might you deploy
>   them?

At the forefront of consideration in Case studies 4.2 and 4.3 is a concern to deliver the best possible outcomes for students. Core values
undoubtedly drive the collegiality illustrated in both these case studies; they also illustrate the challenges that academic leaders face. They
need to address generic leadership capabilities, but also personal credibility, which in large part derives from an individual's ability to listen
and to engage, drawing upon the huge talent within and across the
institution hence my plea for a new approach to academic leadership,
that of 'structured improvisation'.

## SUMMARY

This chapter explored definitions of academic leadership dating back
to the early 1990s to the present day. I suggested that the time is
right for a new approach to academic leadership, with core values
at its heart. Such an approach, which needs to be 'role modelled' by
the most senior of academic leaders, is far more subtle, flexible, and
nuanced according to needs, whilst at the same time taking account
of the external environment. Two perspectives on what it means to be
an academic leader in practice were presented: one from the VP level,
and the other from the VC level. Both stressed the need for appropriate academic leadership behaviours, alongside the need to gain trust,
respect and credibility within one's academic community.

  Finally, is the model of structured improvisation always valid? Are
there times when a different style is necessary – when things go wrong,
or pressures conspire against you? For these situations a sailing anal-
ogy might work well. If things go wrong academic leaders need to
keep hold of the tiller – either tightly or loosely – steering through the
choppy waters, moving towards an engaging vision of the destination
and approximate arrival time. There will be times when academic

leaders have to move to greater structure and firmness of steer according to how choppy the sea. Choppiness can be caused by external or internal factors. Externally, there could be, for example, political or technological imperatives. Internally, there could be financial, or potentially destabilising influences. The trick is knowing when to use different leadership styles and approaches, according to different contexts, to ensure the desired destination is reached. Being agile and flexible allows academic leaders to draw on the expertise of others or, when necessary, take sole leadership, and be more directive, according to the situation. Through greater agility and flexibility, alongside well-honed academic leadership capabilities, academic leaders can enable their staff to gain energy, confidence, and enthusiasm for whatever the future holds.

## FURTHER READING

Gmelch, W. and Buller, J. (2015) *Building academic leadership capacity: A guide to best practices*. San Francisco: Wiley.

Really useful in exploring various developmental interventions to assist transitioning into executive roles.

Goffee, R. and Jones, G. (2009) *Clever: Leading your smartest, most creative people*. Boston: Harvard Business Press.

A fascinating account of how successful leaders retain and deploy the expertise of their most talented staff to good effect.

Marshall, S. (ed.) (2007) *Strategic leadership of change in higher education: What's new?* London: Routledge.

A useful set of case studies illustrating the importance of front-line leadership.

## REFERENCES

Gmelch, W. (2013) *College deans: Leading from within*. Connecticut: Greenwood Press.
Gmelch, W. and Buller, J. (2015) *Building academic leadership capacity: A guide to best practices*. San Francisco: Wiley.
Gmelch, W. and Miskin, V. (1993) *Leadership skills for department chairs*. Bolton: Anker Publishing, 1–2.

Goffee, R. and Jones, G. (2009) *Clever: Leading your smartest, most creative people.* Boston: Harvard Business Press.

Marshall, S. (ed.) (2007) *Strategic leadership of change in higher education: What's new?* London: Routledge.

Middlehurst, R. (1993) *Leading academics.* Maidenhead: Open University Press.

Peters, T. and Waterman, R. (1982) *In search of excellence: Lessons from America's best run companies.* London: Profile Books.

Ramsden, P. (1998) *Learning to lead in higher education.* London: Routledge.

# Part II
# The leadership and management perspective

# 5: Selecting and developing vice-presidents of teaching and learning

## OVERVIEW

This chapter focuses on different approaches to the development of the 'talent pipeline', requiring succession planning for the role of VP (Teaching and Learning) and higher-level roles. Increasingly in the UK, we are seeing such roles advertised in the media, and then re-advertised because institutions are finding it increasingly difficult to engage the right person. Part of the issue is undoubtedly the breadth and depth of the expertise that is required. However, there is the additional challenge that institutions want to recruit executive members who have a proven track record of contributing at the national level. In this chapter, the three stages of the talent pipeline will be explored. Firstly, we will examine the various experiences that assist an academic to move beyond the role of just managing their own teaching load, through to taking on more responsibility. Secondly, we will consider the whole process of recruitment, particularly the use of headhunters and what those aspiring to a senior management role might need to think about when contracting with headhunters. And, finally, we will consider what continuing professional development is necessary so that a VP can keep up to date with changes in both policy and practice, and perform well, achieving the right balance of loyalty to the executive team (i.e. sharing collective responsibility) and to their particular portfolio.

## THE PATHWAY TO BECOMING A VP (TEACHING AND LEARNING)

It would be fair to say that very few, if any, newly appointed academics come into post aspiring to be a VP (Teaching and Learning). By and large, their concern is to ensure that they are managing their portfolio of work, which will not be solely research, teaching preparation, teaching, marking and supervision, but also a range of other citizenship activities, which could include such things as open days, schools liaison and pubic engagement duties. Managing oneself is usually the starting point for any new academic, and once this is mastered, individuals will be in a position to move on to manage other people, be it a research team or taking on responsibility for a programme module, including outside specialist contributors for whom references may need to be checked and an induction prepared.

At some stage, departmental or school responsibilities will be requested of a capable individual, and this is often when tensions start to occur. The request to take on responsibility for chairing the undergraduate teaching committee is really important if you are to progress to a VP role. However, if an individual has not already gained one's own Professorship this could lead to feeling exploited. Fortunately, all UK higher education institutions (HEIs) now have criteria for promotion that include taking on responsibility for teaching and learning. Thus a really talented teacher might consider the next step beyond a role chairing the undergraduate teaching committee to be either a head of department or school or an associate dean with responsibility for teaching and learning. Increasingly institutions are offering developmental training for such roles, which may include coaching and mentoring.

Most institutions expect that a prospective VP (Teaching and Learning) will have carried out the role of dean, and have gained an understanding of the challenges of, for example, quality assurance, curriculum design, digital technologies, and assessment and feedback techniques across a group of clustered disciplines. Once individuals reach this level of seniority, the institution will often deem it important that they undertake some form of leadership development programme, be it in-house or one offered, for example, by the **Higher Education Academy (HEA)** or the **Leadership Foundation for Higher Education (LF)**. It is via this route that the transitioning and step-up to VP becomes easier. This is especially the case when instead of focusing on one's own discipline, one has to work on meeting teaching and learning requirements across a range of disciplines. And, of course, it is the performance in these increasingly important strategically aligned roles that provides academics with experience of change management as responsibility is often delegated down for areas such as **National Student Survey (NSS)** results, employability and recruitment of international students. So a sound understanding of leading and managing change and having the appropriate skillset are crucial. Undoubtedly this expertise will have been acquired earlier in your career – albeit without the great breadth of responsibility that the VP carries with respect to corporate change.

Philip Martin (former pro-vice-chancellor at Sheffield Hallam University) highlights in Case study 5.1 the tensions in terms of the skillset required for a VP role, alongside the difficulties of undertaking the role due to the lack of hard metrics by which to gauge distance travelled or success in teaching and learning other than various **key performance indicators (KPIs)** such as the **NSS**. He thus advocates training and development to introduce academic staff to ways of thinking that they may not have even known existed before, and to ensure that they are capable of making large scale improvements and innovations in practice.

## Case study 5.1: The leadership and management perspective

### Philip Martin, Sheffield Hallam University

What are the primary requirements for university executive leads with the teaching and learning portfolio? And what are their development needs? These questions were at the forefront of my thinking when designing and consulting in the sector on an HEA development programme for deputy vice-chancellors and pro-vice-chancellors new to post, but they also inhabit the minds of a great many vice-chancellors making appointments, for we are looking increasingly to such leaders to produce large-scale improvements and innovations in practice across the university.

The executive lead for education has been radically recast over the last decade.[1] The combined effects of the NSS and the exponentially increasing marketisation of higher education (HE) have produced new imperatives and performance requirements. Where once the university's quality of teaching was an internal affair, realised in the generally vague incarnations produced by a **QA regime**, or by a hotchpotch of evaluation forms, there are now potent performance indicators producing national rankings. Where formerly teaching and learning had only a marginal place on the executive agenda, now it has become central, and determinately linked to key strategies such as estates, IT and finance. The professional requirements have rapidly escalated, and the annual effect of NSS scores on university profiles is potentially volatile, thereby requiring rapid and continuous actions to improve, or at least maintain, the university's reputation. Add to this the radical changes in learning being brought about by new and rapidly developing technologies, and you have a heady mix.

As a consequence, the requisite high-level leadership skills are demanding. PVCs have to produce quick results alongside longer-term strategies. They have to be effective at the executive and inspire confidence at **board** level. Leading an academic community across the disciplinary divides requires sensitivity and determination in equal measure. Commissioning (or writing) a teaching and learning strategy and then leading its implementation is no humdrum task. Those appointed to such roles must develop their capacity to lead and inspire alongside overseeing the increasing professionalisation of teaching and the introduction of cultural change. On a more practical level, they need to be diplomatically adept with a whole range of stakeholders, from students to members of the **council** or **board**, and they commonly have to accomplish their agendas without their own line-management structure, directorate or budget. These abilities are not directly comparable to those required in parallel roles, such as the executive lead on research. While the vocabulary of the person specification may be similar in each case, the job is very different, and fundamentally the difference derives from the levels and kinds of risk in research on the one hand, and teaching and learning on the other. The risks in research, however pressurised, and in some disciplines such as Medicine, massively more consequential, are nevertheless hedged by **peer review**, established research teams, promotional incentives including a career track and relatively sophisticated infrastructures and procedures. The peer review dimension is probably the most important: it offers trusted judgement, support through trial and error, mentoring (informal and formal through, for example, readers' and editors' reports) and it also supplies clear evidence for recognition and reward as well as poor performance. If a colleague aims to produce a **4\*** **journal article** and it is refused first time around, they can have another attempt on the back of the advice received. If a colleague fails in teaching, the NSS and other evaluations are less forgiving and the effects can reverberate well beyond the point of delivery, for teaching rankings tend to be strongly influenced by the point of greatest weakness (student feedback rarely averages such matters out). Furthermore, success in teaching is less easily defined than success in research, partly because the classroom (figurative or real) is still largely private and teachers are working on their own most of the time; and partly because there is no established and trusted currency in good practice modelling. The difference between these two principal dimensions of academic professionalism is stark, and it is precisely this difference which allows there to be a **Research Excellence Framework (REF)** alongside selective research council funding, working by clearly defined criteria and rigorous procedure, and no equivalent for teaching. It should be noted that at the time of writing, preparation to introduce the **Teaching Excellence Framework (TEF)** in England in 2016 is underway. The gap of course, is filled by the **NSS**, with rankings based on bogus differentiation (the **NSS** mark-range commonly extends across only fourteen percentage points).

Altogether, this is an exacting portfolio, and its challenges are not simply localised or institutional. Those taking on the executive lead for teaching and learning also must address the national and international learning landscapes, not only to learn from them, but to contribute to their greater success.

## NOTE

1 Such leads have various titles, most commonly pro- or deputy-vice-chancellor, (Academic/Education/Teaching and Learning/and Student Experience), although sometimes this brief moves beyond the academic experience. Precise responsibilities vary across the UK sector, but broadly such titles indicate the primary institutional responsibility for all taught programmes in the university.

---

### Interrogating practice

1  Consider your preparation for a leadership role (teaching and learning). What does your institution provide in the way of training and development?
2  What do you see as the key elements of the role, for which you would like additional professional development?

## WORKING WITH HEADHUNTERS, PARTICULARLY MAINTAINING CONTROL OF THE SELECTION PROCESS

Addressing the national and international agendas is one of the reasons why more institutions are using headhunters for recruitment of their executive teams. It is not so long ago that the so-called **pre-92** universities offered executive roles internally, on fixed-term contracts. Not only are institutions increasingly recruiting at the top level through headhunters, but they are asking them to find the talent globally to give their strategies the leading edge. Maintaining control of the selection process is crucial, as 'fit', or getting the right person, is essential to ensure effective teamwork that delivers, both within and outside the institution (see Chapter 6).

Peter Mathieson, President of the University of Hong Kong, outlines in Case study 5.2 below the recent recruitment to his executive team, illustrating how the use of a search firm did not involve any loss of control of the recruitment process, providing a case study in effective selection and induction.

> ### Case study 5.2: Selecting and developing pro-vice-chancellors/deputy principals (teaching and learning)

**Peter Mathieson, University of Hong Kong**

*Selecting*

At the University of Hong Kong (HKU), pro-vice-chancellors and deputy principals are invariably subject to global search and therefore a search firm is involved. We have recently completed the search for and appointment of a new vice-president (Teaching and Learning); the post includes being a full member of our senior management team and so I was concerned to address the suitability of the candidates not only regarding their knowledge, experience, capability and ideas about teaching and learning but also in terms of their strategic thinking, management experience, communication skills, team working, etc.

I chaired the search committee, which included the provost, two academic members of staff, a lay member from the university council and a student representative. The candidates undertook an initial paper exercise informed by interviews carried out by the search consultants. Longlisted candidates then underwent Skype interviews (or face-to-face for internal candidates) and thereafter shortlisted candidates were invited to the campus for a formal interview plus meetings with stakeholders from whom feedback was collected.

We prioritised academic credentials, experience in delivery and management of taught programmes, curriculum design/development and review, quality assurance in teaching and learning, innovation, knowledge of international trends, and new methodologies and ideas for the future. Other topics that frequently arose included proposals for objective assessment of teaching excellence, teaching the teachers, motivating researchers to teach and to value teaching, harnessing online teaching internally as well as externally (e.g. **MOOCs**), experiential learning, residential hall culture, integration of students from different countries and cultures. Experience of working in Hong Kong was considered an advantage but was not a pre-requisite. HKU is an English-speaking university.

### *Induction and development*

Any new member of the senior management team will need welcoming and supporting whilst learning the portfolio, especially if they are an external appointee. Active and ongoing engagement with students, teachers, researchers, support staff and external stakeholders should be encouraged. An undue load of committee work or representational duties, especially in the early months of the post, should be avoided. Interaction and sharing with other vice-presidents (VPs) will be vital, both to ensure the new staff member understands their portfolio (research, institutional advancement, **globalisation**, academic staffing) and to ensure teaching and learning is part of the thinking in these complementary areas. New VPs will make an active contribution to strategic planning, particularly for teaching and learning, and also for the other areas including the general development of the university. Continued regular involvement in teaching design and delivery will enhance credibility and keep their feet on the ground. The notion of the VP as a role model for like-minded individuals and as an advocate for teaching and learning internally and externally should be promoted.

Career development is vital. Depending upon the age, experience and ambitions of the individual, the post might be a stepping-stone to those seeking the role of president or other chief executive officer roles. Self-reflection, setting milestones, addressing areas of relative weakness, further development of areas of strength and/or particular interest, regular appraisal and feedback on performance will all help. The primary aim of the postholder, and the criterion upon which success or failure should be judged, should be to deliver effective and substantial progress in the teaching and learning arena for the university, its students and teachers. Success in this domain will open up new opportunities!

---

### Interrogating practice

1   How many of the practices illustrated in the above case study are offered in your institution?
2   Could more be done at the national level to support new VPs? If so, what?

Case study 5.2 provides a really salutary message suggesting that once the recruitment process has taken place the job is not done. Providing sufficient space for a new member of the executive team to adjust – particularly when transitioning to their new role, where collective responsibility is a given – is crucial. The approach Mathieson offers is helpful: do not overburden new recruits with too much committee work or activity that does not permit sufficient time to get to know their working colleagues, or simply to ask how to go about getting things done and, indeed, how 'things are done'. Having said this, most VPs would agree that to maintain one's credibility, it is important to keep one's hand in through programme development and/or some teaching. This can prove really difficult given the demands of the role, but does ensure student contact beyond just the Students' Union representatives.

## CONTINUING PROFESSIONAL DEVELOPMENT FOR VPS

Once in the role, how do VPs ensure that they keep up to date with the ever-increasing developments, including policy, technologies, etc.? In Case study 5.1, Philip Martin referred to an external developmental programme, but what about ongoing support?

At the HEA, we host a biannual 24-hour **PVC network** event, based on current topics that VPs have requested. The network offers collaborative mentoring and co-coaching opportunities. Increasingly, a range of continuing professional development programmes is offered to support VPs in staying up to date and also in transitioning into a role.

Development programmes for executive team members are typically external (e.g. those run by HEA, LFHE, Harvard, INSEAD, Oxford Said). Coaching, mentoring or representing one's institution or the sector on external committies all help. In the chapter on building and developing effective teams, which follows, one VP refers to her role chairing a national committee as powerful in terms of providing high-level leadership experience with the opportunity to learn about what is taking place across the rapidly changing landscape of HE.

Action Learning Sets (ALS) are often incorporated into leadership development programmes, and often continue after the programme finishes, thereby providing the continuity to apply one's new learning. Typically, an ALS comprises approximately six people from different institutions, with an additional suitably qualified person acting as the facilitator. They abide by the Chatham House rule (i.e. nothing may be attributed to members of the ALS in discussion outside the meeting, unless explicitly agreed by those concerned) along with other ground rules determined by the set. The ALS methodology provides an opportunity for those involved to take it in turn to present their real time issues and challenges, inviting questions and probing from the rest of the set to help the 'presenter' gain greater clarity and see the issue through the eyes of others. Increasingly, the facilitator assists in focusing down on a set of scenarios to move forward, ultimately helping the presenter to identify courses of actions. The facilitator then rotates to the next presenter, repeating the process. Ultimately, all the ALS members leave with a commitment to action (which may be 'no action', in those cases where the individual just has to accept the situation). This co-coaching process also affords the opportunity for each member to reflect on the success or otherwise of actions from previous sessions.

Coaching has become increasingly popular with executive team members as it provides an opportunity for a VP to benefit from external help to assist them in unpacking an issue and determining possible ways forward. Most HEIs now have their own internal team of coaches, and the executive team are normally able to access the skills of well-qualified and accredited external professional in the field too. A good coach will help the VP, through facilitation, to explore an issue, consider the context, current situation, culture and key actors, and come up with a range of possible routes forward and then determine a course of action. Facilitated thinking time is something that in the past was often seen as a luxury. However, in today's rapidly changing and complex world, it is clearly crucial that executive staff make time for such reflective activity.

Another aspect of development that many VPs have found useful is that of mentoring whereby a more experienced person or senior person with a broadly similar executive role undertakes to meet with the VP periodically to encourage them to both think about and take steps towards their next role. Case study 5.3 considers just that: the various developmental activities that assist VPs to not only develop in their role, but also to be a highly competent player in the collective role of the executive team.

## Case Study 5.3: Continuing professional development and encouraging new vice-chancellors

### David Phoenix, London South Bank University (LSBU)

Whilst it may appear to be stating the obvious, I think it is important for the university and applicant to be clear about what is being offered at the point of selection. As vice-chancellor, what are you are seeking in terms of experience, skills and behaviours and what are you offering? Others may disagree, but it is my belief that to be successful at this level you need someone who is highly able as an individual but who is also able to work as part of a leadership team. This is a two-way process and so the applicant should ensure they select the team they want to work with. Membership of a university senior team is a true privilege and incredibly rewarding, but it can also be exceptionally challenging. To flourish, you need to buy into the vision and culture, feel supported to develop as an individual, and feel you can make a contribution to the institution's goals – not all PVC roles are the same. Make sure you spend time with those who might be your future colleagues and, if you can, speak to staff and students about their experiences.

Once you are in post, there are a number of development areas to consider: firstly, understanding your role as part of the team. With my team at London South Bank University, I use tools such as **RACI** (responsible, accountable, consulted, informed) charts and **MBTI** (Myers Briggs Type Inventory) assessments to enable the team to debate responsibilities and engage in discussion about behaviours and approaches. These tools provide ideal vehicles to get the team to understand each other's roles and ways of thinking. I expect my executive to be clear about their responsibilities, to support each other and not to work in silos. I usually encourage staff to attend a senior leadership programme; these help present new ideas on strategy development and implementation but in my experience they have two greater benefits. The first is they help a new PVC to establish a network of experienced individuals. The second is you find out, from a leadership perspective, that there is much that is similar across a wide range of institutions, so you can learn from other people about what constitutes success or failure and then apply this to your own situation.

Secondly, you need to understand your role at your new university. For those PVCs with true vision and leadership skills, the PVC role provides an incredibly exciting and, at times, challenging opportunity. Teaching and learning is a fast-moving area with the development of **blended learning**, consideration of topics such as **learning gain** and debate about knowledge versus skills, internationalisation, and linking teaching and research. Whilst PVC roles vary across the sector, one thing tends to be common: unfortunately, many staff adapt to new pedagogic developments at a much slower pace than one would like! At LSBU our teaching and learning strategy clearly expects the creation of a learning pathway. The challenge for the PVC is ensure this becomes a reality rather than simply a description. In so doing it enables them to influence the learning environment in a way that can affect the lives of many thousands of students as well as the staff in professional and academic areas. They need to therefore conceptualise this and develop a delivery model. To take this agenda forward, I believe it is important to look at external network development. Key bodies to consider are the **HEA, JISC** and the **Leadership Foundation** but there are also opportunities to engage with groups such as **UCEA** to learn about staff development activities that have been undertaken elsewhere and to look at how issues such as union engagement and workforce planning have been approached. When undertaking visits to other organisations, I would also consider including private providers and commercial groups such as **Pearson** or **IBM** to see what developments they have been undertaking. Indeed at LSBU initial interactions with IBM led to a major partnership in the development of the digital learning environment and **learning analytics**. This external engagement is vital to maintain currency and to bring new ideas into an organisation. It provides a vehicle to increase the profile of the university and provides evidence for yourself of impact outside the university, which is something you would expect from those seen as high-performing. It is important that this is supported.

Finally, in any role there is a need to have a sounding board for issues you may not wish to discuss with colleagues. Each member of my executive is therefore provided with an executive coach in their first six to twelve months. This is an experienced individual who can facilitate their thinking and provide thought pieces and studies to enable them to develop their approach to leadership and management. This can be helpful in considering new situations such as engagement with the board or other stakeholders. Staff also will quickly see through the insincere or disconnected if they do not feel the engagement is real. It is not just what you do but how you do it. Such coaching provides an opportunity for you to gain 360° feedback from colleagues so you can consider an honest assessment of how you are perceived and how you may need to modify your communication style to enhance impact.

---

Case study 5.3 explored a number of approaches to developing the capabilities and currency of VPs, to enable them to add value to the executive team as well as open up further possibilities beyond the role of VP.

### Interrogating practice

1 Which of the developmental activities highlighted in Case study 5.3 have you engaged with? To what effect?
2 What does your personal development plan look like? Are there any other developmental activities, as a result of reading this chapter, you are going to add to your plan? If so, describe these.

## SUMMARY

This chapter has outlined three very different perspectives on the selection and development of VPs. All three leaders are passionate about the need to get the right person in post because they need to be capable of taking on some significant pan-institutional change programmes, alongside culture change and, in the case of the UK, ensure a high profile and positioning in league tables. All three highlight the importance of VPs working on strategy development, learning through engagement with their top team colleagues, and necessarily interacting with the corporate estates, finance and information systems teams, etc. Executive leadership programmes, coaching, mentoring and ongoing support are seen to be crucial. Further to the types of continuing professional development highlighted here, it is worth VPs asking their chief executives what support is available, which may come through the appraisal and feedback process. VPs should remember that despite the challenges, there are plenty of developmental opportunities, with probably the largest being the various national and international networks, offering the opportunity to explore and test new ideas. It should be an exciting journey!

## FURTHER READING

Breakwell, G. and Tytherleigh, M. (2008) *The characteristics, roles and selection of VCs*. London: Leadership Foundation for Higher Education.

Despite being focused on vice-chancellors, this publication provides fascinating insights into the widespread use of executive search agencies in the talent-spotting, interviewing, longlisting and recruitment of executive staff. Potentially helpful to aspiring VPs.

Ketteridge, S., Marshall, S. and Fry, H. (2002) *The effective academic*. London: Kogan Page.

This book provides an overview of the different levels at which success-ful leaders in HE have to operate: managing the external environment, running the business, creating intellectual wealth, and, engaging with the digital chalk-face. Additionally, a whole section is devoted to developing career-long competence, and how this manifests itself in universities.

Smith, D., Adams, J. and Mount, D. (2007) *UK universities and executive officers: The changing role of the PVC*. London: Leadership Foundation for Higher Education.

Although somewhat dated, nevertheless interesting in placing the role (i.e. job description, responsibilities and expectations) in the wider context of the whole university, and HE more broadly.

# 6: Building and developing effective teams

## OVERVIEW

Vice-presidents (Teaching and Learning) who have either developed, or are developing, their **graduate attributes** frameworks to embed in their institution's curricula, know only too well how important it is for students to understand how to work effectively in teams. However, further to the exploration in Chapter 4 on academic leadership, it appears that working in balanced, non-heirarchical teams is not always easy to achieve be it amongst students or academic staff. This chapter does not rehearse the literature on teamwork with which many readers will be familiar, be it Belbin (www.Belbin.com) with his team roles typology, Kouzes and Posner (2007) with their work exploring how to improve and empower teams, Katzenbach and Smith (1993) with their analysis of the factors contributing to high-performing teams, or Tuckman (1965) with his stages of team development. Instead, this chapter seeks to understand how, when there are few if any carrots to encourage academic staff to engage in upping their game with respect to teaching and learning, we can inspire them to work more effectively as teams. VPs (Teaching and Learning) are required to operate in a range of different teams such as the Executive team, possibly their own team of direct reports (though a good number of VPs do not have any resources, being termed 'policy VPs'), and possibly a team of assistant deans with responsibility for Teaching and Learning (with this group line managed, and therefore accountable to, the faculty deans who may make competing demands). At the same time there are so-called 'teams' which come in the form of committees and working groups (the latter increasingly called 'task and finish groups').

This chapter therefore explores the differing roles that the VP (Teaching and Learning) has to play in these differing teams. In some, they are not the leaders, in some they are **primus inter pares**, and in some they definitely are the leader. Irrespective of the team, it is the VP (Teaching and Learning) who is accountable for delivering the results as identified in the teaching and learning strategy of an organisation, which is often the embodiment of a set of year-on-year ambitious **key performance indicators (KPIs)**. Each of these team roles are explored below, through examination of firstly, the executive team; secondly, the formal teams that the VP chairs; thirdly, the informal teams that the VP interfaces with; and finally, external teams.

## THE EXECUTIVE TEAM

Much has been written about executive teams, including questioning the ability of such teams to perform as anything other than a group of highly capable, driven and determined individuals. Their behaviour in the executive team may well be the result of their personal ambition as they navigate their own route to a top leadership role. This in itself can cause problems as a number of members may see themselves as being in competition with colleagues for the next available top job. Kennie and Woodfield (2008) undertook a useful study examining the different types of higher education (HE) top team behaviour, noting that most executive teams are groups of highly effective independent specialists. In conversations with VPs, it is most disconcerting to hear that a good number suggest, still, that VPs (Teaching and Learning) are the 'poor relations' in executive teams, and that they find it difficult to find a voice. It has also been posited that perhaps this is a gender issue:

> You have to have a fully rounded academic profile (engage in research and L&T) whereas a leader in research isn't expected in most institutions to demonstrate their scholarship in L&T. You need thick skin (particularly if you are a woman) and be able to counter others' ideas with well-reasoned arguments that are informed by critical thinking. If you do not, you are dismissed.

At best, the executive are a team who hold to the notion of **collective responsibility**, and will support each other to deliver the best possible outcomes and greatest impact for the student body. At worst, they will be dysfunctional, and more concerned with personal achievement, which fortunately, these days, is usually rapidly addressed by the president or vice-chancellor, who is accountable to the chair of the board for the collective performance of the executive. So, what can you do, personally, to assist in encouraging highly-effective teams, focused on the task of bringing about the best possible learning experience for your students?

Firstly, you have to know how best to hold your own in the executive. Tom Kennie, who undertook (with Steve Woodfield) the research referred to above, has worked with many executive teams across the UK, facilitating team working and also coaching individual members of the team. He outlines his observations, based on his experience of working with such teams, in Case study 6.1. As with earlier tips and techniques, Kennie recommends being 'visible' and 'engaged'– not just with one's own portfolio, but where the different executive portfolios overlap (e.g. estates, HR, IT), so as to exploit synergies to the benefit of the whole institution. Vice-chancellors expect collective responsibility for the achievement of key targets. Therefore each member of the executive team is responsible for building a range of relationships to gain full understanding of the complexities of the present learning landscape and how these might be addressed.

## Case study 6.1: Building effective teams

### Tom Kennie, Ranmore Consulting Group

You have been a highly successful dean, internationally-known researcher or passionate innovator in some area of educational development. Then one day you wake up and you are now a PVC/vice-principal with responsibility for teaching and learning. You have a relatively clean slate on which to write and you are also now a member of the senior team, in fact it is the top team. What an amazing opportunity and privilege. What's not to like about your promotion?

It is now six months since you took up your new role. The realities are starting to be apparent. In your previous role you had a relatively large budget to deploy. You also had quite a large team to manage. You could decide what to do in the morning, delegate specific responsibilities by lunchtime and leave at the end of the day feeling that you had set things in motion. Now it feels all so different. Your budget is tiny, you have no direct reports, and delegation in the way you did it before does not seem to lead to any action. Then there is the top team. 'Team' does not feel like the right term either. One of your fellow team members took you aside and helped you understand the difference. She said (using a football metaphor) that she started off as a mid-fielder passing the ball to her fellow team members. Rarely was the ball returned, most times it was simply kicked into touch, off the field. She then had a eureka moment when she realised she was using the wrong metaphor. This was more of an athletics team – one that seemed solely interested in jumping higher and higher (mainly in the league tables), another was obsessed with speed, running faster and faster (mainly to get more international students) whereas another was more of a boxer (mainly throwing their weight around, particularly about regulations and policies). Sounds familiar?

Leading a cross-cutting theme, such as Teaching and Learning in a top team, demands a somewhat different approach from that demanded when you are leading an academic unit. In this new role you are most definitely leading primarily 'beyond authority' whereas in the old world it was primarily about leading 'in authority'. Likewise, this top team often carries out large parts of its work together as a group of highly-effective independent specialists. What is, however, crucial is that it is clear on what and when it must act with team discipline (i.e. in accordance with cabinet responsibility). The best top teams think through and identify what their team agenda is; most do not, and it sounds as if you are in one of those types of team. So how do you manage to transition into this new top team role? Think about the following five key issues:

1  **Vision**. Be clear what your ambitions are in relation to teaching and learning. What are the priorities for you and collectively as a team? Be careful about trying to please everyone. Is our collective ambition to be, say, more technologically enabled in our teaching and learning? Or more pedagogically skilled? Or more employability focused? Or is it to develop more globally

engaged students? Try and create commitment to a limited but clear, collective agenda.

2 **Visibility**. It is all too easy to sit at the centre developing strategies and policies, feeding the committee paper machine. Much more demanding (and effective) is to be visible and engaged with the core of the academic and professional communities and, even better, routinely engaged with the student body.

3 **Values**. A significant part of your role is to articulate, model and engage the team in living the educational values which demonstrate your genuine commitment to an exceptional student experience. You also need to be the educational conscience of the team, challenging actions and decisions which do not align with those values you have agreed matter most. Are we sure that our desire to increase the number of firsts and 2:1s is absolutely about our commitment to student success and not being driven for the prime purpose of increasing our league table performance?

4 **Vary**. To work in this new top team and to have influence across the institution will require you to vary your leadership style from that which you deployed previously. You will need to work through influence, build coalitions, develop your boundary-spanning leadership skills and capacity.

5 **Vocal**. Finally, you have to be heard. You need to be a vocal supporter and cheerleader about successes in teaching and learning. Celebrate good practice and incentivise this through awards for innovations and for those who are role models and demonstrate leadership in some aspect of teaching and learning. To really be effective, however, you also need to have a voice on all of the other major issues on the top team's agenda. You need to contribute to other strategic issues – from research to internationalisation, enterprise, partnership development, and financial sustainability, among many others.

If you and your fellow team members pay attention to these issues, then the chances of developing an integrated and coordinated teaching and learning strategy which is able to be delivered and sustained will be heightened significantly.

> **Interrogating practice**
>
> 1 To what extent do you find the sporting metaphor referred to in Kennie's second paragraph apposite to your situation?
> 2 How well integrated is your institution's teaching and learning strategy with other sub-corporate strategies? How do you monitor the effectiveness of the cascade of information and actions?

## FORMAL TEAMS THAT MUST BE CHAIRED BY THE VP

As alluded to in Case study 6.1, varying one's style is crucial to operating successfully in different teams across the institution. The overall teaching and learning committee is a key organisational body which sets the tone for the rest of the infrastructure for both discussion of and determination of tactics to deliver the teaching and learning strategy. In the survey of VPs, four key challenges were alluded to: managing semi-autonomous professionals with a range of expertise; understanding different disciplinary cultures; keeping abreast of the constantly changing external environment and political drivers; and finding time to continue to teach, in order to have credibility. The way that they endeavoured to address these challenges was to model the behaviours the leader wanted staff to emulate. The four main skills identified were: communication and engagement, respect, listening and patience, and negotiating and influencing (drawing in others to achieve a shared vision on how best to deliver their institution's mission with respect to the educational aims).

The cascading down from the institution's teaching and learning committee flows to a range of other committees. The key instrument for ensuring joined up alignment of the delivery plan are the faculty teaching and learning committees (often chaired by faculty associate deans) and below that, the school and departmental teaching and learning committees.

Too often it is expected that once **KPIs** and tactics are cascaded down, everything will follow naturally and results will be achieved.

But remember Kennie's advice: the VP needs to be visible. It is wise to attend various teaching and learning committee meetings to get a sense of the quality of the discussion. Ask yourself, 'Do the local performance indicators and tactics align with the values and overall thrust of the corporate strategy?' Having this level of visibility will enhance your credibility with staff. It will also demonstrate that a member of the executive really values hearing what those at the student interface have to say about the approaches being promoted. And, as one survey respondent noted:

> Being enthusiastic and sharing that enthusiasm about driving up the quality of the students' learning experiences is important . . . [alongside] encouraging and sharing innovation.
> (Survey respondent, autumn 2014)

So, beyond these formal mechanisms for formulation and delivery of corporate strategy, there are a range of informal networks and teams with which the VP can usefully engage, to ensure that the full community – staff and students – are able to contribute with energy and enthusiasm, and are provided with a voice with respect to the direction of travel and appropriate tactics. Case study 6.2, offered by Debra Humphris, Vice-Rector at Imperial College, outlines a well considered and proven approach to bringing together the whole university community as a team.

## INFORMAL TEAMS WITH WHOM THE VP INTERFACES

In Case study 6.1, the various informal teams are kept in touch with policy development and delivery options through a range of both face-to-face and digital approaches, thereby allowing everyone to be part of the team. The model used at Imperial College has additionally encouraged a distributed leadership approach in that individuals (including students) who are particularly keen to lead on different aspects of the ambitious strategy, are encouraged and supported to rise to the challenge. Such an approach is one that facilitates a coherent team spirit; no-one can complain that they have not had the opportunity either to showcase their own ideas or to lead initiatives for which they believe they have particular expertise.

## Case study 6.2: Leading teaching and learning in HE

**Debra Humphris, University of Brighton, formerly Imperial College London**

Within the community of universities there will always be a range of motivations that engage colleagues and students in the development and delivery of the education offer and the wider experience of students. In taking on the important role of leading the development of strategy for education and the student experience, you have an opportunity to engage the community of your institution, to enable the talents and ideas of that community to play a vital role to create a team-based approach to improvement.

To illustrate this point, this case study describes the process by which the community of Imperial College engaged in shaping, agreeing and implementing our Education and Student Strategy.

### Context

Imperial College London is a world-class university based in a vibrant globally important city, with a reputation for excellence in education and research. Our reputation is based on our world-class staff and facilities, and our work is underpinned by a dynamic, enterprising culture. Core to our mission is the delivery of a world-class education that enables our graduates to take their distinctive set of knowledge and skills and apply them for the benefit of society. Our graduates develop excellent technical and practical skills based on a thorough grounding in one of our core disciplines and go on to use their talent and ideas all over the world in their chosen careers.

### Imperial College Education and Student Strategy

The strategy development process was deliberately designed to bring together the community, as a team, both to shape and take a role in implementation. The process involved multiple means of engagement, web-based consultations, open town hall meetings, all designed to enable members of the college community, students and staff to contribute ideas and comments. There were four phases:

1 **Contributing ideas.** Staff, students and alumni were invited to contribute their ideas and views based on four draft strategic objectives. To encourage engagement, a number of provocations were provided, including links to external websites to related developments from universities across the globe. It can become all too easy to focus on the familiar so the provocations encouraged colleagues to look up and look out. The feedback from this phase was used to shape the next stage of the process.

2 **Discussion paper.** Building on existing good practice and informed by responses to the first phase, a green discussion paper was developed. It set out a number of potential actions, identified as either 'core' or 'desirable'. The community was invited to comment and to identify their top priorities from the list of desirable actions.

3 **Draft strategy and implementation plan.** Informed by the responses to the discussion paper, a draft strategy paper was discussed by the Management Board in June 2013 and the strategic objectives were endorsed. In September 2013 the provost's board endorsed an implementation plan and reporting process.

4 **Programme delivery.** Key to the achievement of the strategy is a managed programme of implementation; reflecting again the same ethos as the development process and involving as many members of the community as possible. The leadership of specific actions has been taken on by colleagues from across the college, with active student involvement in all areas.

From the outset, the implementation plan was always set as a three- to five-year process, enabling sufficient time for action and giving a deadline for change.

The Education and Student Strategy can be viewed at http://www.imperial.ac.uk/education-and-student-strategy (accessed 22 August 2015).

Implicit in Case study 6.2 is the concern to develop and build a collaborative and team approach to bring about strategy development, promoting ownership by individuals and aiding strategy delivery.

---

### Interrogating practice

1   How do you test ideas that you believe will have a positive impact on the student learning experience, e.g. new feedback approaches?
2   How do you get staff and students involved in shaping ideas into plans for action?

---

Clearly, a VP needs to have competent chairing skills to lead committee work, working groups or task and finish groups. The highly effective chair will be mindful of Tuckman's (1965) stages of team development i.e. forming, storming, norming and performing, facilitating progress and pacing each of these four stages. Also, an effective chair will ensure that within any team discussion, everyone has a voice, irrespective of where their preference is on the introversion–extraversion personality spectrum. Nominating sub-teams to go away and consider some suggested scenarios for moving forward is another way of ensuring that team members work across boundaries. Such an approach promotes a greater understanding of the different lenses through which the diverse parts of an HEI view teaching and learning.

## EXTERNAL TEAMS

But, of course, strategic development does not happen in a vacuum. Case study 6.2 illustrated the need to encourage staff and students to 'look up and out'. VPs are required (as noted in the spate of recent job descriptions for the role) to be involved in external benchmarking, in key national (and international) networks and, where possible, lead external working groups. Why is this important for a VP? Profiling of your own institution is a key aspect of student recruitment, and once the VP has addressed the challenges of their first year, and are confident that both the infrastructure and personnel are operating as they would wish, they can move to this next level of looking up and out. Engagement in external teams, be they by mission, issues (e.g. improving student engagement) or national policy initiatives, can provide real kudos for an institution whilst giving the VP insights into how other institutions operate. Case study 6.3, contributed by Sue Rigby, Vice-Principal of the University of Edinburgh, highlights the importance of teams at three levels: firstly, the institutional, where she notes that 'teams ultimately speed the plough', citing the £3 million student support services initiative as an example of a team 'passing the baton' according to relevant expertise. Secondly, at the UK-wide level, since she chaired a national-level committee which sought to determine the information needs of postgraduate students (this may not have delivered the result that had been originally anticipated but was based on a consultative process and sound evidence base); and thirdly, an internationally recognised new approach to soft project methodology. In all instances, she illustrates the values of mutual respect, recognition of different types of expertise, ownership, and commitment to success.

## Case study 6.3: Building effective teams – a personal case study

### Sue Rigby, University of Edinburgh

Taking a leadership role in teaching and learning in most universities requires the key attribute of being able to work beyond authority (Middleton 2007). This requirement can be partially met, or at least some of its inherent challenges addressed, through team building.

Teams take time to build. Once developed, it still takes effort to explain strategic thinking to a team, and patience to allow team members to explore, critique and develop these ideas. It can be tempting in a leadership role to avoid this commitment, especially where quick change is required. I would argue that this shortcut is never justified. Teams ultimately speed the plough and the time invested in their formation and maintenance is always well spent.

Why are teams valuable and what are they for? Below I list a slightly eclectic set of reasons for building effective teams as part of the leadership portfolio concerning teaching and learning.

These paraphrase some of the established mantras around team functions, but are processed through personal examples and experience.

1 **Teams engage all the stakeholders who matter.** They will almost always include senior managers, academics, professional service staff, and students. As such they ensure that all voices are heard and all solutions ground-truthed through a variety of perspectives. The team that I chaired, working through **HEFCE** to consider the information needs of taught postgraduate students, included a wide-range of stakeholders from academic institutions and bodies that oversee or report on them. It was able to consider and reject the idea of a universal student survey for postgraduates but was able to suggest a practical approach to information provision that satisfied all those involved and is now implemented across the UK.

2 **Teams ensure that ideas are tested before they are applied.** Anyone who voices concern or is critical of a plan can be invited to join the team. That way, their views are aired and considered, dropped if they are foolish or developed if they are sound. Plans at the University of Edinburgh for a personal tutor system were developed by a team of the academic and support staff who would ultimately operate it. Concerns and worries, particularly around the confidentiality of the student/ mentor relationship, could be addressed at an early stage and a satisfactory conclusion reached.

3 **Teams can provide expert leadership for all stages of a project, not just its origination**. By building a team with multiple and complementary talents, a project can be scoped, initiated, undertaken and assessed to the highest standards, which is a set of skills no one person brings to bear equally. A £3 million project to enhance our student support services has gone through creative development, thoughtful implementation and successful evaluation based on the respective strengths of members of the leadership team overseeing the project. New services for students, such as a single portal for all enquiries and enhanced induction and communication, have been possible because of this baton-passing of capacities within the team.

4 **Teams can generate developments that are not originally envisaged.** In terms of their original purpose and their mode of working. For instance, we developed a soft-project

methodology, with an emphasis on **appreciative inquiry (AI)**, soft skills and ongoing dialogue, which is now being used internationally and outside the HE sector. This was because one of our project teams recognised that our existing methodologies (based on IT and construction projects) didn't fit with the way we needed to work on delivering qualitative and **culture change**. This initiative gave us confidence in our working methodology, but it was not considered when the steering group formed.

Put crudely, teams engage the troublesome, expunge bad ideas, improve rushed or poor planning, form a **sandpit of creativity** and ensure that all bases are covered. It is well worth taking the time to create and maintain your creative teams, even in the fastest developing situation.

## REFERENCE

Middleton, J. (2007) *Beyond authority: Leadership in a changing world.* London: Palgrave Macmillan.

Rigby's analysis is a compelling and eloquent argument for team working, but remember that her case study is focused on effective teams. Ineffective team leadership – however well meaning – can completely undermine all those benefits, as highlighted above.

### Interrogating practice

1 What different teams do you lead? How does the composition of each differ?
2 How do you build and develop your teams to ensure that the 'whole is greater than the sum of the parts'?

Case study 6.3, as with the example offered in Case study 6.1, once again illustrates that 'chairing' skills are crucial. An effective chair person sets the right tone and engages teams in a culture of continuous development, providing the appropriate conditions for everyone to thrive. The skilful deployment of chairing skills enables every team member to develop their own knowledge, skills and capabilities at the same time as gaining an appreciation of the unique contribution that different functions within the HEI provide.

## SUMMARY

In this chapter we explored how best to operate within a range of teams, not solely the executive team. The challenges and tensions between the different members of the executive team will always be there, as each person fights to gain the best chance of not just delivering the **KPIs** associated with their portfolio but exceeding their targets. Developing the team to function well is not only beneficial for the existing team, but helpful in preparing executive team members for their role as team leader. The chapter then explored the range of other teams with which the VP should aim to engage in order to empower others, distribute leadership, and ensure that their institution is well positioned not just in their own nation's HE sector but internationally. A common theme throughout the chapter was the need to both build and develop the team, taking the lead in role modelling and bringing out the strengths and expertise of different team members. Effective chairing skills were highlighted as being essential for a VP; attending one of your institution's workshops on this key skill is highly recommended.

## FURTHER READING

Katzenbach, J. and Smith, D. (1993) *The wisdom of teams*. Boston: HBR Press.

Useful for considering how best to challenge teams to perform at an ever higher level, whilst maintaining loyalty and engagement.

Kennie, T. and Woodfield, S. (2008) '"Teamwork" or "working as a team"? The theory and practice of top team working in UK HE', *Higher Education Quarterly*, 62(4): 319–436.

A useful exploration of UK HE top-team working and its challenges, exploring the different teams the executive team members have to interface with, and providing a range of useful suggestions.

Kouzes, J. and Posner, B. (2007) *The leadership challenge.* 4th edn. San Francisco: Jossey Bass.

Useful for revisiting the five practices of exemplary leadership, this book emphasises the relational nature of leadership and the importance of trust at all levels.

## REFERENCES

Belbin, M. Available from www.belbin.com (accessed 13 August 2015).
Katzenbach, J. and Smith, D. (1993) *The wisdom of teams.* Boston: HBR Press.
Kennie, T. and Woodfield, S. (2008) '"Teamwork" or "working as a team"? The theory and practice of top team working in UK HE', *Higher Education Quarterly*, 62(4): 319–436.
Kouzes, J. and Posner, B. (2007) *The leadership challenge.* 4th edn. San Francisco: Jossey-Bass.
Tuckman, B. (1965) 'Developmental sequence in small groups', *Psychological Bulletin*, 63(6): 384–399.

# 7: Managing performance

## OVERVIEW

Managing performance is a key aspect of the role of any VP. Effective performance management requires strong and credible leadership to bring about a culture of sustainable high performance. Performance management has a poor reputation generally, particularly in higher education (HE). It requires strong advocates and role models at senior levels of leadership, who overtly support and practise sound processes such as those illustrated in this chapter.

The range of performance measures for VPs (Teaching and Learning) are perhaps the most diverse and far-reaching of any of the executive portfolios, as suggested by the respondents of the UK VP survey. All mentioned **key performance indicators (KPIs)** such as **entrance tariffs**, **progression data**, external examiner reports, **QAA** reviews, **degree classifications** and graduate level destinations/ destination of leavers as KPIs against which they were appraised. There were repeated suggestions that year-on-year progress against baseline data was expected, primarily via an annual percentage uplift. Constant monitoring of targets and progress against targets is a feature of most UK higher education institutions (HEIs). Most of these indicators of successful performance (or otherwise) are usually monitored by an institution's teaching, learning and student experience committee, and measured through annual performance against operating plan in reports to the **board**. The prospect of the **Teaching Excellence Framework (TEF)** in England, linked, with its suggested link, to an institution's ability to charge higher fees, puts performance management even more into the foreground. Delivering these metrics is not just about process but inextricably linked to the culture of the institution.

Cascading KPIs or targets down to the faculty and school level requires deans (or their delegated responsible people, i.e. associate deans for teaching and learning) and heads of school (or their delegated responsible people, i.e. directors of Teaching and Learning) to engage in a range of negotiations to determine which KPIs are appropriate for the different parts of the institution. Such discussions need to be held fairly, transparently and equitably involving all staff. They need to be seen as part of the psychological contract or deal to deliver the institution's mission. For example, entry tariffs may vary from faculty to faculty, dependent on market supply and demand and trend analysis. Staff should be encouraged to use systematic data for critical benchmarking against other faculties, within the institution and across competitor institutions.

Finally, the KPIs or subset targets are cascaded down to individuals. This is where a variety of techniques are being deployed across different institutions as a means of incentivising and motivating staff to up their game. Strategic approaches to encourage improvement are an important consideration for VPs (Teaching and Learning), with creative approaches articulated in many institutional teaching and learning strategies. Pump priming funding for developing innovative approaches to teaching, shadowing, exchanges and educational development workshops are increasingly used to ensure that these targets are met.

This chapter looks in more detail at how exactly the process of ensuring performance in teaching and learning can be well managed. We then move on to explore negotiating targets, and then finally address a more holistic approach to managing operational performance via data which feeds up from individuals, through to school and faculty level, to enable VPs to monitor and analyse institutional progress.

## MANAGEMENT OF TEACHING AND LEARNING PERFORMANCE ACROSS THE INSTITUTION

Most performance expectations are embodied in institutional teaching and learning strategies, which set out clear **KPIs** and targets. It is the responsibility of the VP (Teaching and Learning) to negotiate these with deans, usually in one-to-one meetings, prior to school annual reviews. The school operating review is an annual event whereby results from the previous year are examined and projections for the following year negotiated. Such a process is common in many institutions now, and involves central (e.g. the VP) and faculty (e.g. the dean and assistant deans) representation, with school representation (head of school accompanied by their leadership team, which includes the director of teaching and learning). It is through this process that feedback on performance against the **KPIs** is obtained at different levels, which then informs the annual reviews of individual members of staff. Additionally, based on current performance against targets, new targets will be set. This is the stage where, at one end of the spectrum, celebrating success can be an outcome or, at the other end, remediation suggested.

Tim Stewart, Dean of the Business School at BPP University, argues in Case study 7.1 that role modelling and clarity of goals are the best ways of managing performance, alongside having difficult conversations as and where appropriate.

## Case study 7.1: Managing performance

### Tim Stewart, BPP Business School

BPP Business School is one of the four schools of BPP University, a private provider focused on practical business education to support employability and career advancement. The business school aims to adopt a professional outlook towards education and professional standards are at the heart of its culture. The business school has grown rapidly over its first few years and now has more than 3,000 students. A key ingredient in its success is establishing and maintaining a strong performance culture.

1  **Staff recruitment and selection.** In addition to the traditional assessment of expertise, great emphasis is placed on recruiting staff with the appropriate professional values and attitudes to work effectively in a high-performance culture. This includes a willingness to take direction and feedback, to work collaboratively with colleagues, to demonstrate a strong work ethic, a can-do mindset and an innate desire to get things done.

2  **Staff support: induction, training and coaching.** High staff performance goals require the school to strongly support its staff. The business school runs a range of online and face-to-face

induction activities for staff. The school encourages academic staff to undertake our PG Certificate in Professional Education and obtain recognition from the **Higher Education Academy (HEA)**. Non-academic staff are also encouraged to learn and gain further qualifications. All staff are expected to attend regular training and professional development activity and there is a strong ethos of helping everyone within the team to succeed. Senior managers play mentoring roles with more junior staff.

3 **Clarifying minimum acceptable performance levels.** The school sets clear minimum expectations for teaching performance, **digital literacy** and responsiveness to students. Everyone is given support to be able to achieve the minimum standards.

4 **Managers leading by example.** Managers are expected to set a good example in regard to the professional behaviours and attitudes expected of all staff. We aim to demonstrate we have a professional approach to education and so professional dress, responsiveness, punctuality and strong customer service are important for us.

5 **Clear goals and priorities.** Every member of staff has formal annual objectives, quarterly priorities that are reviewed regularly, and clear job descriptions which are reviewed annually. Every single person receives an appraisal and feedback, and informal one-to-one contact with a line manager is a regular and valued occurrence.

6 **Team meetings and communication.** We place a strong emphasis on bringing together teams within the school to work together to solve problems and to exchange ideas. Successes are recognised and celebrated together.

7 **Responding to underperformance.** Everyone is expected to perform well in their role and this is especially important in activities directly impacting student experience. Where an individual is not performing well, the team tries to support them and help them improve their performance. If performance cannot be improved, the underperformance is not allowed to persist but is dealt with. Employee morale, engagement and performance are high because long-term underperformance is not a feature of the school culture. The use of minimum standards is helpful in clarifying where the line for performance intervention lies.

Setting the minimum standards is difficult for institutions which have never done so before. However, they have to start somewhere, and with the range of metrics by which VPs are now judged (and tasked to achieve), it would be a rare institution that did not have some baseline data from which to determine the next year's targets.

---

### Interrogating practice

1 What are the minimum standards that are set for your teaching staff? How are they determined?
2 How are staff supported in not only meeting but exceeding these baseline standards?
3 What happens if staff do not achieve these minimum standards or exceed these minimum standards?

---

## NEGOTIATING TARGETS

Increasingly in annual reviews, deans and heads of schools are involved in negotiating targets to be achieved over the forthcoming year. Recruitment targets, improvement in particular **National Student Survey (NSS)** scores, progression rates – all these feature in the range of targets that are regularly reviewed and negotiated, further to determination by the VP.

Ian Dunn, VP at Coventry University, outlines in Case study 7.2 the negotiation of targets at the individual level as a key means of achieving the university's ambition.

### Case study 7.2: The leadership and management perspective

**Ian Dunn, Coventry University**

> If you are instead trying to educate a broader spectrum of the population, including elite students, and you aren't using analytics, you won't know what's going on.
>
> (Michael M Crow, EDUCAUSE Review, 2012)

Coventry University re-launched its ambition to be recognised, amongst other attributes, as a leader in the teaching and learning field. This work started in 2010 with a focus on the course of study and the students as active collaborators. The university took the view that in order to be recognised as a leader in the field we needed to understand where we were, what our students thought and then be capable of making change. In order to do this we recognised the need for relevant data capture so that we could create a baseline and measure the impact of activities undertaken.

Coventry University carries out the evaluation, at a central university level, of each of the subjects that we teach. The results consist of a set of quantitative responses and also a free text section. The results are presented very quickly to a module tutor and to their head of department. Each tutor is then asked to post a response to the key findings, on the **virtual learning environment (VLE)**.

The university then aggregates this data to look for trends in performance, or underperformance, in subject areas and also in different student groups. We believe that this mechanism gives us both a baseline and a way in which we can look at whole university performance.

The data gathered is incredibly rich and allows a range of analysis. It allows us to experiment with changes to assessment and feedback, teaching and learning, personal development, course organisation and learning space design and development. Being able to assess the broad impact of a change against the baseline is a powerful tool.

The university introduced, as a part of the performance and development review of all staff, a measure related to the satisfaction of students in teaching and learning. This is a hard metric around recovery or excellence, depending on the situation. This is a very clear and direct link between performance and the voice expressed by students in evaluating the quality of the taught experience.

Coventry University strongly believes that the whole university sector needs to become much more adept at handling large volumes of data about the teaching and learning agenda. In order for this to be seen as having relevance it must be linked to individual and team performance. This connection needs to be made alongside a major phase of empowerment. It is unacceptable for the university centre to hold all the data and then to judge on this basis. Coventry University tries to democratise this information by presenting the data associated with each course in the form of a dashboard.

In summary, and to echo the words of Michael Crow, if we do not take seriously the need for strong metrics we will never properly understand the impact of the measures that we take.

## REFERENCE

Crow, M. (2012) '"No more excuses": Michael Crow on analytics', *EDUCASE Review*, 47(4). Available from http://er.educause.edu/articles/2012/7/no-more-excuses-michael-m-crow-on-analytics (accessed 21 August 2015).

---

Data, which should include **learning analytics**, is becoming a really powerful tool for the ongoing monitoring of student progress and outcomes. Additionally, data can highlight trends and the impact of the various contributory factors to successful learning outcomes. Also, hard data can provide the evidence base against which performance can be judged. Nevertheless, undertaking such sensitive discussions was highlighted as an aspect of the role of VP that was worrisome, according to the survey of VPs that was undertaken to inform this book. Despite many universities now offering workshops on handling sensitive conversations, it is clearly an area where VPs would like some key pointers. Strong metrics offer a sound evidence base which can inform and depersonalise discussions. Some ideas for managing such conversations, which provides a framework for making progress, include:

1   Focus on the evidence, not the person. Ask questions such as 'What does the evidence suggest?' 'What was going on here?' Stick to the facts.
2   Engage in joint problem solving. 'What interventions might we deploy to address this issue?' 'What are our competitor schools/faculties doing to address similar issues?' 'Who needs to be involved?'

3   Determine mutually agreed targets and deadlines. 'What are real-
    istic targets?' 'How might we monitor progress: over the short
    term, medium term and long term?'
4   Explore an appropriate change strategy. 'Given the target and
    deadline, how is this going to be achieved?' 'What will be your
    first step?' 'What might potential barriers be?' 'What help might be
    beneficial for you?'
5   Agree dates for future meetings to monitor progress. 'What is a
    realistic date to meet again to ensure the agreed intervention is
    delivering what is required?'

---

### Interrogating practice

1   How are targets strategically aligned in your institution?
    What particular **KPIs** are core to the range of discussions
    at the faculty, school and individual levels?
2   What range of metrics and **learning analytics** do you use
    to monitor performance? Are they sufficient?

---

## HOLISTIC APPROACHES TO ASSURE OPERATIONAL PERFORMANCE

As stated earlier in this chapter, higher education institutions (HEIs)
in the UK have moved towards more holistic approaches to ensure
that faculties and schools are delivering institutionally determined
**KPIs**. By and large, the approach has been to introduce an annual
planning cycle which includes a process, usually taking place in the
autumn, which reviews the previous year, to include the whole basket of KPIs. The University of Arizona has introduced an on-going
logging system, Vitae, with the expectation that all staff will feed in
the relevant performance data as and when received. VPs (or other
senior leaders) are able to access a 'dashboard' to see where the
institution is placed at any point in the year and to slice the data in
a way that is appropriate to them (e.g. research publications at the
faculty or discipline level, ).

Tom Millar, Vice Provost of the University of Arizona, explains in
Case study 7.3 how he supported academic staff to deliver the UA
Vitae online system – a holistic faculty reporting system into which

staff have to enter ongoing data, particularly around scholarship, service and outreach work. This information is not just used at the chalk face, but it also feeds into accreditation, programme reviews, and other reports used for planning and budgeting.

## Case study 7.3: University of Arizona Vitae

### Tim Millar, University of Arizona

What is UA Vitae? The UA Vitae online system was introduced to provide data to inform the annual reviews of faculty and continuing-status professionals. The system draws on existing databases for information on faculty members' teaching, work history and grants. The UA Vitae provides a paperless annual review process that saves time as it can serve a range of purposes.

Who benefits from the system? Everyone does as it reduces the need for multiple entries of data for accreditation, program reviews and also allows faculty to fill in gaps to provide a more complete picture of **scholarly and service activities**.

Why introduce UA Vitae? Because most sources of data do not adequately represent faculty members' scholarly and creative work, especially in areas such as the Humanities where scholarship is often published in books not indexed by the **Scival system**. Faculty members' service and outreach efforts are not recorded in any existing source. These efforts are vital to documenting faculty members' broader impact. Faculty are able to use UA Vitae to provide information on their outreach and service efforts and verify their information on their teaching, publications and other activities. This information can then be used in accreditation, program reviews and other reports for planning and budgeting.

Into the future for UA Vitae and qualitative data. **Peer reviews** of teaching are being introduced as a collaborative process of inquiry, further to our introduction of outcomes assessment, to provide both a baseline and a guiding philosophy for reflecting upon how we assess teaching. Adopting the **peer review** process as an integral part of the work of faculty members is also a move to bring about greater parity of esteem between research and teaching.

It has been agreed that all such assessments must be multi-perspectival, and include input from students, self-reflections and **peer reviews**.

**Peer reviews** are fundamental to all the professional work of academic staff. For them to be done well, they need to have well-defined protocols that include student evaluations, reflective statements on teaching philosophies and criteria for assessing the classroom interactions that are vital to student engagement.

If we can understand **peer reviews** to be as integral to teaching as they are to research, we may be able to build communities of practice around teaching comparable to the collaborative venues that sustain our research work.

From such a perspective, we can see that the outcomes to be achieved in assessments of teaching are not simply to improve student learning but to build the **peer review** culture around teaching that is so vital to the collaborative process of learning from and through our research. This is UA's next challenge.

---

### Interrogating practice

1  How are staff in your institution encouraged to log evidence of the full range of their academic outputs?
2  How is this information used? Are there lessons that can be learned from Case study 7.3 as to how such information can assist the overall performance of your institution? If so, which particular aspects?
3  How might you incorporate some of these ideas into the practice of your institution? And for readers based in England, which ideas might you incorporate to assist with the delivery of the **Teaching Excellence Framework (TEF)** to be introduced in 2016?

## SUMMARY

In this chapter, the notion of both leading and managing performance was considered. It included an exploration of a set of core principles to underpin threshold standards of performance in the area of Teaching and Learning such as staff recruitment and selection, subsequent induction and development, role modelling appropriate performance, setting clear goals and priorities, and enabling two-way communication flow. Moving beyond the qualitative, the chapter explored quantitative means of managing performance. With the advent of a range of metrics and **learning analytics**, a more objective approach to the evaluation of performance is provided at all levels: the institutional, faculty, school and individual levels. And finally, the chapter explored an approach which placed responsibility for monitoring one's own individual performance electronically through an ongoing logging system. Such an approach included encouraging **reflective practice**, as well as providing a rich data source for the university to draw on for the **peer review** of teaching. This approach was used in the University of Arizona's drive for parity of esteem between research and teaching, led by the VP. Recording of metrics in individual portfolios, which can subsequently be 'mined' at the faculty and corporate levels, is worth exploring, along with all the other best practice examples highlighted in the three case studies. Such approaches will undoubtedly have a part to play in the development of the **Teaching Excellence Framework (TEF)** in England, where performance management will become even more important to the role of the VP (Teaching and Learning).

## FURTHER READING

Buckley, A. *et al.* (2015) *HEPI-HEA Student Academic Experience Survey.* York: Higher Education Academy.

This survey has been undertaken annually every spring since 2006, and is most useful for trend analysis, particularly when looking at students' views on a range of areas that fall within the responsibility of the VPs and assistant deans (Teaching and Learning). For example, it investigates the teaching and learning experiences of students, including:

- satisfaction with courses
- reasons for dissatisfaction
- experience of different-sized classes
- total time spent working
- perceptions of value for money
- institutional spending priorities
- student wellbeing.

Cashmore, A. *et al.* (2013) *Rebalancing promotion in the HE sector: Is teaching excellence being rewarded?* York: Higher Education Academy.

A sound, practical read which builds on previous reports by surveying progress in the HE sector with regard to approaches to the reward and recognition of learning and teaching excellence. Should prove useful to VPs looking to reward excellent leaders of teaching and learning. More than 70 case studies from 55 institutions were collected, covering a range of individuals, institutions, disciplines and career points. Several barriers to effective reward and recognition are identified and recommendations for future development in this area are presented.

Cranfield School of Management (2014) *Performance management in UK higher education institutions: The need for a hybrid approach.* London: Leadership Foundation for Higher Education.

This publication compares different approaches to performance management, arguing that different contexts demand different approaches, e.g. performance managing *research* performance presents a different requirement to performance managing *teaching* performance. The publication offers a useful perspective that is explored in more detail in the case studies.

## REFERENCES

Cashmore, A. *et al.* (2013) *Rebalancing promotion in the HE sector: Is teaching excellence being rewarded?* York: Higher Education Academy.
Higher Education Academy and Higher Education Policy Institute (2015) *2015 Academic Experience Survey.* Oxford: Higher Education Policy Institute. Available from www.hepi.ac.uk/2015/06/04/2015-academic-experience-survey (accessed 10 August 2015).

# Part III
# Engendering a
# change culture

# 8: Leading change

## OVERVIEW

Strategy development and delivery is a key feature of every VP's role, as illustrated in a number of case studies in Chapter 1 of this book. It is inextricably linked to the leadership of change. The process starts with a vision, then a gap analysis, to determine what needs to change, leading on to determine an appropriate strategy for change. Translating this strategy into action is the true test of a leader's ability. This chapter outlines some tried and tested models and techniques for leading and managing change, including illustrations of different approaches.

Leading and managing change is a constant in terms of any organisation's practice – be it changes in staff, operations, finance, etc. The focus of change is on specific, desired outcomes. This chapter concentrates on leading change as opposed to leading transitions: the two are subtly different. The focus of a transition requires consideration of how to leave the past practice behind, i.e. letting go of something, so as to adopt new behaviours. This notion is explored more in Chapter 9. Instead, this chapter will focus on the nuts and bolts of leading change.

Most prospective VPs will have led a number of change initiatives during their careers, but perhaps not at the pan-institutional level. In the survey of VPs undertaken to underpin this handbook, a key challenge that most participants alluded to was being expected to bring about step change in response to a range of requirements aimed at enhancing the development, delivery and profile of teaching and learning. The case studies offered in this chapter focus on three different aspects of change that all higher education (HE) providers are grappling with. Firstly, the need to improve **digital literacy skills of staff**, to be able to provide an enhanced technological learning environment for the student population, is explored. Secondly, an introduction to constructive alumni engagement (beyond financial giving) through a series of projects designed to enhance the student offer is outlined. And, thirdly, HR policies which recognise and reward a commitment to and uplifting of teaching and learning are described. HE institutional leaders tend to adopt three different approaches to change: step change, incremental change, or policy driven change. These will be considered in the sections which follow and in addition an overall framework for mapping proposed institutional change is offered in Table 8.1.

All three approaches offered in the following case studies feature the four key steps of the planning phase as identified in Table 8.1, i.e.:

**Table 8.1** Thirteen pointers for leading institutional change (Marshall 2007)

| Phase 1<br>Planning stage<br>1–7 | 1 | identify what needs to change |
| | 2 | develop a clear vision |
| | 3 | determine the leadership of the project (to include a clear articulation of the goal which needs to be achieved) |
| | 4 | identify the significant steps in the change process |
| | 5 | avoid undue haste |
| | 6 | determine how to align people behind the change (identify change agents and resistors) |
| | 7 | inspire confidence by forestalling problems (**contingency planning** and determining a communications plan) |
| Phase 2<br>Actioning the plan<br>8–11 | 8 | distributed leadership (building teams at different levels of the organisation, thereby developing trust and being mindful of the different speeds at which individuals internalise the need for change) |
| | 9 | ongoing and constant communication (explaining, listening, ensuring understanding, questioning, guiding, acknowledging feelings and seeking ongoing feedback) |
| | 10 | involving people at all levels (to seek and develop commitment, participation, motivation and ownership) |
| | 11 | seeking out and celebrating early successes. |
| Phase 3<br>Monitoring and<br>evaluating impact<br>12–13 | 12 | learning from experience (what works well, what does not work well, what would we do differently next time); |
| | 13 | planning for continuous improvement (something that is essential in the rapidly changing learning landscape). |

- being clear not only about what needs to change but being clear as to why change is needed (the 'why' question);
- offering a compelling vision of what success will look like (the 'what' question);
- allocating well-defined roles, responsibilities and accountabilities (the 'who' and 'how' questions);
- determining an action plan with clear milestones (including named responsible personnel) to be achieved along the way (the 'when' and 'by whom' questions).

## STEP CHANGE: TECHNOLOGICAL CHANGE TO SUPPORT ENHANCED STUDENT LEARNING

In the case study which follows, in preparation for the first cohort of students coming in as undergraduates paying £9,000 per year tuition fees in September 2012, the executive team recognised that there needed to be step change to justify the near trebling of the tuition fees. This, they believed, necessitated a significant uplift in the institutional offer for students. A strategy was determined starting with a gap analysis that highlighted the step change required to ensure that students' virtual learning experience was 'state of the art'and that all staff utilised the student learning portal as standard. It was decided that the best way to achieve this was to discuss what success would look like in September 2012 (when the first undergraduates paying £9,000 p.a. would be commencing their studies) and work backwards from there. A clear vision of what students should be presented with, in terms of their learning environment, was articulated by the pro-vice-chancellor. Sub-leaders were appointed to lead the various strands of the enhanced provision. The case study below is a good illustration of the various phases of a well-managed change process.

> ### Case study 8.1: Newcastle University's student offer

**Steve Williams, Newcastle University**

> We provide students with . . . opportunities to develop their knowledge and skills for life, learning and work: to succeed

in their studies, to meet personal and professional goals and aspirations, and to equip them for success after they graduate.

(Newcastle University Student Offer, 2011)

Newcastle University's student offer sets out what an undergraduate can expect from their time with us. Our website's ambitious commitments relate to teaching, pastoral support, facilities and technologies. To put this programme in place, keep it running, enhance it and roll it out further are significant challenges for the leadership of the organisation. Done well, we have effective teaching, motivated staff and satisfied students. The risks – staff overload, poor technology and staff and student dissatisfaction – are clear.

This is how we addressed it:

Early in 2011, the pro-vice-chancellor (Learning and Teaching) convened a group to plan the student offer for September 2012. A unified approach was promoted, with the technology going hand in glove with the pedagogy. Some universities have competing lists of priorities – a list of IT projects and a separate list of pedagogical improvement projects with IT implications. We realised early on that a single programme was essential, along with a programme management[1] approach to deliver it.

A project officer, responsible for the published schedule work, was made accountable to a steering group. Each development in pedagogy or technology could be traced back to a commitment in the student offer. For example, we did not deploy hundreds of rooms of lecture capture because it is cool technology, but to deliver enhanced revision and reflection opportunities to thousands of students. Monthly scorecards for each project made governance transparent.

Each project was collaboratively worked on by practising academics and by technology experts, so each idea was both pedagogically appropriate and technologically doable.

By September 2012, the programme delivered the offer. This included well-formulated, research-informed programmes, clear assessments, pastoral support and a wide range of learning technologies. Our eLearning and Student Information Group then took responsibility for continuing the work, chaired by a senior academic, with academic, technologist and student members. Reporting to this group are working groups for each area – **virtual** learning environments (VLE), lecture capture, the student app – so that we can track the changing needs of our students.

Since 2012 we have recast the student offer in the context of our international and partnership operations. We offer a comparable experience for students on our Malaysian medical school and Singapore engineering programmes.

We are currently looking at how our online and **blended learning** programmes, informed by our first **MOOCs** on the **FutureLearn** platform, can reflect the same principles.

What made this an unusual challenge for the leadership of the organisation?

- many diverse stakeholders: every student and every academic
- the need to balance standardisation with respecting academic freedom
- multiple technologies
- a one-off programme and a continuing service as well as further enhancement.

Across the university, we use the 'technology at the right hand of the academic activity' approach. The process of submitting Newcastle University's **Research Excellence Framework (REF)** return worked in a similar way and was praised by the REF assessors.

To summarise, the programme management approach worked well. Student feedback is very positive and it is clear that the leadership vision behind its success was crucial.

## NOTE

1 Definition of programme management from the Cabinet Office, UK Government: 'the action of carrying out the coordinated organization, direction and implementation of a dossier of projects and transformation activities (i.e. the programme) to achieve outcomes and realize benefits of strategic importance . . . ' https://www.axelos.com/msp

## REFERENCE

Newcastle University Student Offer (2011) Available from http://www.ncl.ac.uk/quilt/assets/documents/str-newcastle-offer.pdf (accessed 12 August 2015).

Case study 8.1 illustrates a marked step change further to a clear vision and clear leadership; to include distributed leadership. There was clear **stakeholder mapping,** determining key players to get full buy-in and engagement, to use their power to influence the process and the outcome. In this instance, students were central to the determination of key success factors. This is an essential part of any change process, to ensure that no constituencies are left out that could, eventually, sabotage the change. In this case study, there was sensitive determination of who the different steering group members and different working group leaders and members should be.

> ### Interrogating practice
>
> 1 How does your institution keep apace with technological advances and the needs of students?
> 2 When putting together a new programme, or reviewing a programme, which 'experts' are involved in exploring how best to achieve learning outcomes, and what is the unique contribution that can be made by the different learning support experts?
> 3 Could your institution do better? How?

## INCREMENTAL CHANGE: USING ALUMNI TO ENHANCE STUDENT EMPLOYABILITY

In the next case study, a key challenge for the university was identified: how to increase and enhance the employability of graduates. It was determined that better use of alumni could deliver a distinct lifting of graduate employability, and a range of initiatives were developed and trialled. An *incremental* approach to change management was adopted, with the different strands, as in Case study 8.1, led by different constituencies of the university. Like Case study 8.1, the focus was results-orientated. The leadership of this initiative, coming out of the VP's office, required significant investment in those constituting the **guiding coalition** (Kotter 1996): members of the careers service, student support services, the recruitment offices and the alumni office. Once again, there was clear, detailed planning prior to actioning so that the impact of this staged change could be felt from early on. Rather than determine a go live date for the whole initiative, the focus was a range of metrics to evaluate success, including 'take up' and the leavers' destination returns.

## Case study 8.2: Alumni engagement

### Chris Cox, University of Manchester

For many years (arguably decades) alumni programmes in the UK talked a good game in terms of potential ways in which alumni *could* support institutional strategies around recruitment, the student experience and employability, with insufficient resource or focus to actually make it happen. The combination of the introduction and subsequent significant increase of tuition fees, growing competition for the best students, an increased focus on student experience and employability and their associated national ratings, has encouraged a number of universities to develop innovative ways to engage alumni far more directly and meaningfully in student experience projects than had previously been the case.

At the University of Manchester we narrowed this down to five or six programmatic areas where we could develop substantial and tested engagement opportunities which could be tailored to the needs of academic units while drawing on central data and advisory capacity. This would allow us to learn from experience, benefit from efficiencies and economies of scale (especially around information management), and avoid re-inventing the wheel each time for specific departments. Our priority programmes since 2011/12 have focused on:

- online career profiles of alumni linked to specific courses aimed at both prospective and current students, demonstrating the range of career options that may be open to graduates of specific courses (with a focus on challenging stereotypes and received wisdoms);
- one-on-one careers mentoring, via rapid expansion of the well-established 'Manchester Gold' mentoring programme;

- 'Meet the Professionals' sessions, where five or six selected alumni return to engage and challenge dozens of current students from specific courses as to how they might think about and prepare for their futures;
- visiting speaker events, engaging selected alumni in a combination of curricular and extracurricular seminars and presentations, ranging from MBA seminars through to reflections on business ethics for our flagship university-wide student volunteering programme;
- a new donor-funded 'Global Graduates' programme, through which widening participation students have had the opportunity to travel internationally to meet alumni in the workplace, reflect on the global opportunities that may be open to them, and learn about transnational and local cultural norms and expectations in the workplace and beyond.

We have tracked progress both in terms of numbers of alumni participating across these programmes (well over 1,500 in 2013/14), the numbers of students benefitting (harder to measure, but well over 3,500 in 2013/14), and student feedback (extremely positive across the board, especially for 'Meet the Professionals', with 95 per cent+ positive feedback now the norm).

We are still at the foothills and have a great deal more to do. While causal links will always be difficult to prove in this kind of work, we hope over time to be able to demonstrate genuine impact on both **National Student Survey (NSS)** scores and the employability of our graduates, both in terms of their first job, but also – critically – their second and third.

Our experience so far suggests that four factors are key to success: firstly, you need robust, well-run programmes run by careers, student services or recruitment offices with colleagues ready to engage with alumni, to work collaboratively with the alumni office and to ensure a positive experience for those volunteering their time. (As for charitable donors, alumni are making a voluntary investment. They need to understand that their time and experience is valued and treated with respect if we want them to continue their support and build on it.) Secondly, you need good quality information on your alumni – what they studied, when, where they are now, current role and career trajectory, and how they want to be contacted and engaged. That only comes if alumni/student volunteering is seen as a core component of a wider alumni communications, information and engagement strategy. That in turn links to the third factor: investment. The Manchester executive team has invested in the Development Office in a meaningful manner over the last eight years because it genuinely saw the importance of this wider alumni engagement, beyond financial giving, and how important both cash and volunteering commitments would be to the university's future. And finally, we learned quickly that we need be more selective when inviting alumni to volunteer with students than we do when asking them to make charitable gifts – we are after all placing them in a position of responsibility and influence with our students in a way that is not typically the case with charitable gifts.

Focus, organisation and investment at Manchester provided a foundation for the creation of a results-oriented suite of practical programmes that attract excellent and appropriate alumni and connect them with motivated students. The learning experience is enjoyed by all involved and the measurable success of the programmes now provides a positive impetus for further expansion and refinement.

---

### Interrogating practice

1  When looking to deliver student success, what particular metrics feature in your institution?
2  When contemplating any change, who else might you look to, to provide you with an uplifted and distinctive approach, as illustrated in Case study 8.2?

## BRINGING ABOUT WHOLESCALE ENGAGEMENT WITH THE TEACHING AND LEARNING STRATEGY: POLICY APPROACH

The next case study illustrates an approach where a policy driver underpinned the impetus to change. The identified change was further to a gap analysis revealing that the recognition and rewarding of commitment to teaching and learning, alongside the equality and diversity agenda, was undermining fair play. These dual challenges will be recognised by many readers. In this next case study one can see a real determination to tackle workforce development and to embrace inclusivity (of gender and of promotion criteria for dual track promotions). The outcomes – after only seven years – offer an impressive testimony to the leadership of UMass Lowell's chancellor, Martin Meehan.

## Case study 8.3: Involvement in teaching and learning – advancing academic careers

**Jacqueline F. Moloney, University of Massachusetts Lowell**

UMass Lowell has undergone a dramatic transformation over the past seven years under the leadership of Chancellor Martin T. Meehan. There is much evidence that supports this statement including the fact that the standard bearer for college ranking in the US, the US News and World Report, elevated the institution by 27 spots in just four years to one of the top 100 public universities and among the fastest rising in the nation. The institution has grown by over 40 per cent while increasing selectivity by 80 points on the Scholastic Aptitude Tests (SATs) in just the past five years; ten new buildings have been added over the same timeframe.

One of the cornerstones of the university's success is a strong commitment to improving teaching and learning and advancing those academic leaders who advance it. This commitment has led directly to the advancement of academic leaders who have pursued careers in teaching and learning, especially for women. In fact, in the senior cabinet, nearly 50 per cent of the members of the academic team are women who have been promoted to associate dean, dean, associate provost and executive vice-chancellor, primarily because of their early career involvement in initiatives around innovation related to improving teaching and learning.

There are three major strategic initiatives that have been adopted to foster this culture.

1 **Institutional commitment to teaching and learning.** There are numerous ways the institution fosters excellence in teaching and learning. First, is its prominence in UMass Lowell 2020, the institution's strategic plan which is framed by five pillars of excellence, Transformational Education being the first. The pillar encourages the entire campus to engage in the expansion of experiential learning opportunities, innovation in academic support, teaching with technology, the integration of entrepreneurship in the curriculum and assessment of student learning.

2 **Excellence in teaching and learning supported and rewarded.** A committee of twenty faculty oversees the university's Transformational Education strategic plan, which is co-chaired by a dean and an associate provost, both women, who rose from the ranks of faculty. The committee identifies strategic initiatives on an annual basis aimed at improving teaching and learning and student retention.

   Those initiatives include seed grants that enable faculty to experiment with and integrate innovation in the areas outlined above. There are numerous professional workshops held in various formats throughout the year including a 'Fridays with Faculty' luncheon that enables faculty to share best practice with colleagues.

   The committee convenes an annual symposium that features many of the faculty's accomplishments, and is widely attended. The faculty present posters on innovative strategies, which encourages colleagues to adopt the innovations whilst publicly acknowledging emerging leaders in the faculty.

3 **Professional advancement** Since the university is going through such a period of rapid growth, there has been more opportunity for professional advancement for faculty seeking administrative careers. The university has systematically balanced an approach to promoting from within as well as hiring externally. As a result, of the Academic Council of Deans and Vice Provosts, eleven of its twenty-four members (almost 50 per cent) leaders have been promoted from the faculty within the past five years. Seven of the eleven are women and/ or minorities. It could be said that most were promoted in some part for the expertise and leadership in advancing and improving teaching and learning: expertise fostered by the experiences outlined above.

In summary, there are numerous methods by which universities and colleges can advance by purposefully supporting the development of those faculty committed to teaching and learning. UMass Lowell's capacity to rise in the rankings provides one example of an institution that has accomplished this and the case study hopefully offers strategies and insights on best practices.

---

### Interrogating practice

1  How does your institution encourage and bring about change? (E.g. in the case study above, seed grants were offered.) Could more be done? If so, what?
2  How does your institution celebrate success – not just at the end of a successful change project, but along the way?
3  How are staff recognised and rewarded for their part in change process. Could more be done? If so, what?

## SUMMARY

The case studies above offer responses to real-time challenges that institutions have recently faced: providing a digitally enhanced learning environment for students, addressing the need to uplift students' employability, and addressing the need for changed HR promotions policies to recognise and reward staff commitment, excellence in teaching, equality and diversity. Although the approaches to change – including the series of steps or action plans – vary, readers will, I am sure, have appreciated the amount of time spent planning and mapping out suitable courses of action (and noted the resonance with the pointers outlined in Table 8.1). All three institutional change initiatives were successful, with success being achieved through visible academic leadership combined with distributed leadership, which promoted the engagement of the whole institutional community.

## FURTHER READING

Kotter, J. (1996) *Leading change*. Boston: Harvard Business School Press.

If readers have not read this classic, which has been updated a number of times, this book highlights and illustrates Kotter's 8-point approach to leading change, summarised below:

1 ceate urgency
2 form a powerful coalition create a vision for change
3 create a vision for change
4 communicate the vision
5 remove obstacles
6 create short term wins
7 build on the change
8 anchor the change in corporate culture.

Marshall, S. (ed.) (2007) *Strategic leadership of change in HE: What's new?* London: Routledge.

This text represents the first text providing an overview of key pointers for HE institutional leaders to consider when looking to bring about change, via the thirteen pointers, alongside a number of other easy to use approaches which derived from the UK wide one-year change projects supported by the **Leadership Foundation for Higher Education**. Many of the case study chapters in this volume are still relevant today and include: a conversational approach to quality, approaches to enhancing an individual's performance, developing scholarship in a teaching-intensive university, equality and diversity, and developing and embedding global perspectives.

Moss Kanter, R. (2012) 'Ten reasons why people resist change', *Harvard Business Review*. Available from https://hbr.org/2012/09/ten-reasons-people-resist-chang (accessed 21 August 2015).

Another classic, with the premise being that leadership is about change, yet what is a leader to do when faced with ubiquitous resistance? Resistance to change manifests itself in many ways, from diffidence, foot-dragging and inertia to petty sabotage or outright rebellion. The best way that leaders of change can manage this is to understand the predictable sources of resistance and ensure that a staged approach to mitigating these barriers is determined. The author gives ten reasons for resistance by those who feel they are being 'done to':

1 loss of control
2 too much uncertainty
3 surprise, surprise
4 everything seems different
5 loss of face
6 concerns about professional competence
7 more work
8 the ripple effect
9 past resentments
10 genuine feelings of threat.

## REFERENCES

Kotter, J. (2002) *The heart of change: Real-life stories of how people change their organizations.* Boston: Harvard Business Press.

Marshall, S. (ed.) (2007) *Strategic leadership of change in HE: What's new?* London: Routledge.

# 9: Leading transitions

## OVERVIEW

Leading and managing change – as explored in the previous chapter – requires a basic skillset for anyone in a management or leadership role. Taking people with you, and helping them to let go of old patterns of behaviour, is critical. Failure to let go can result in change initiatives going awry hence the importance of exploring the leadership of transitions, which engages with both the cognitive and the affective domains. Bridges (2009) refers to the three stages of transitioning as firstly, helping staff let go of the status quo (or part of it); secondly, moving into a neutral zone (celebrating an ending), and finally, moving into the new beginning. Additionally:

> The transition management plan differs from the change management plan in several ways. First, it is much more detailed, addressing the change on the personal rather than the collective level . . . Second, it is oriented to the process and not just the outcome. It lays out the details of what's going to be done to help those individuals deal with the effects of the change. It tells them when they can expect to receive information and training, and how and when they can have input into the planning process . . . [and third] a change management plan starts with the outcome and then works backwards step by step . . . A transition management plan, on the other hand, starts with where the people are and works forward, step by step, through the process of leaving the past behind, getting through the wilderness and profiting from it, and emerging with new attitudes, behaviours and identity.
>
> (Bridges 2009: 67)

UK higher education (HE) policy over the last five to ten years has made a fundamental impact on learning and teaching strategies, placing the student or learner at the heart of the HE experience. New funding regimes, new legislation and now, in England, the new quality assurance approach and the prospect of the **Teaching Excellence Framework (TEF)**, have made it even more critical to bring about transformational change in teaching and learning processes and outcomes. HE staff are having to re-conceptualise their roles. This chapter aims to ensure the reader has the key tenets of the different factors which contribute to success in leading transitions – bringing about new attitudes, behaviours and identity – as opposed to just delivering changes in approach.

The three case studies in this chapter are all focused on bringing about holistic **culture change** across the authors' universities. Each illustrates the use of different models and techniques that will assist the reader in considering how best to engage the hearts and minds of their own staff, and determine which techniques (or combination of techniques) might assist with a mapping exercise to gain staff engagement.

The chapter is organised according to three broad strategic approaches to transitioning, identified in an earlier piece of work (Marshall 2007):

- led from the top, with a clear change architecture determined by an executive-led steering group;
- growing from the ground, utilising the **snowball effect**, i.e. initially working with the innovators, and then gaining momentum in the wake of such piloting;
- the incentivised approach, where 'carrots' – usually financial – are offered to encourage staff to engage.

These three case studies exemplify the desired outcome of providing enhanced student learning provision. The first illustrates a pan-university move from three- to four-year undergraduate degree programmes; the second is about exploiting new technologies for student learning; and the final case study outlines a six-year campus estates redevelopment project. Each used a range of techniques to ensure stakeholders (e.g. staff and students) were engaged and moving to the desired vision. Success in all three initiatives was underpinned by a clear vision and exceptional leadership, combined with a well-thought- through programme to assist staff and students transition to the new value proposition regarding their institution's teaching and learning offer. All three planned for in-built and ongoing support for staff and to ensure that the transition did not falter.

## A TOP DOWN APPROACH, ENGAGING STAFF TO ENSURE SUCCESSFUL TRANSITIONING

In the case study which follows, an approach to delivering a key national policy initiative – moving from a three-year degree to a four-year degree – is outlined by Amy Tsui, then deputy president for teaching and learning at the University of Hong Kong (HKU). Often a top down approach derives from a crisis (often financial), or an external imperative, requiring delivery within a fixed period of time. In the case of UHK, this initiative derived from a political decision with a fixed date for implementation. Since this was such an all-encompassing project, Tsui needed to determine a comprehensive 'architecture' which would facilitate engagement from staff at all levels, to bring about effective delivery of the goal by the go live date.

> ### Case study 9.1: Leading transitions – the case of undergraduate education reform at HKU

**Amy B. M. Tsui, University of Hong Kong**

Why don't you just tell us what to do?

In 2005 I was tasked with the responsibility of steering the reform of undergraduate education from three years to four years, which was mandated by the Hong Kong government to be implemented in 2012. A rough framework for the reform was drafted after a number of informal conversations with a range of staff. During one of the sessions, a professor stood up and said, with great sincerity, 'Why don't you just tell us what to do? That will save a lot of time!' My answer was, 'I wish I could do that, but I don't have the answer. I need your help in envisioning what changes are needed, and how we can bring that about.'

Whilst change has been referred to as something external that the leader wants to bring about and transition has been referred to as the internal psychological reorientation that is necessary for change (Bridges, 2002), I would argue that transition is not just a process of psychological re-orientation; it is a process of co-construction of vision and goals between the leader and the led; it is a process of gaining ownership of change. In this sense, transition is an integral part of change.

> I have been teaching for over 20 years, and my students love my teaching. Why change?

This was a response from another professor during consultation that typified reaction from another quarter of the university. Subsequently I did two things. First, I presented the big picture: the rapid changes brought about by technology globally, the demands made on HE, and how higher education institutions (HEIs) elsewhere have coped with these demands. Seeing the big picture is crucial to effecting transition as it takes people beyond the narrow confines of their day-to-day work to see the significance of their work in a bigger context. Benchmarking against international best practice is an effective means of making people realise that they can no longer rest on their laurels.

Second, I presented evidence for change through a number of large-scale longitudinal surveys of various aspects of the curriculum and student learning experience. The findings were disseminated widely and served as the basis for deliberating why and what changes should be made. Confronting people with evidence for change is a disconcerting process during which the initial reaction is typically skepticism about the validity and reliability of the data. However, *sustained* evidence is a powerful means of moving people out of their comfort zone as it forces them to come to terms with the findings and think of ways to address them.

> Why do we need six or seven years' planning for just an additional year?

This was another reaction from members of the university when planning for the implementation of the new degree system started. We decided from the beginning that instead of planning for just the additional year, we should review undergraduate education holistically and, if necessary, make fundamental changes. We realised that we should not underestimate the time needed to co-construct a common vision and educational goals, and the complexity of aligning professional and non-professional faculties. We must allow:

- for variation in the pace and extent of alignment amongst and within faculties;
- flexibility in adapting, whilst holding on firm to basic goals and principles;
- time for innovative ideas to emerge and be piloted, for reviewing failures and for subsequent refinement.

It is commonly believed that leading change involves setting well-defined goals and laying down a clear implementation plan with milestones and timeline, complemented by a good communication plan. But I believe leading change is not a unidirectional process of the leader communicating to staff what needs to be done and what the outcome should be. Effecting change is a joint enterprise between the leader and the led. It is a process of transitioning from old to new which allows for negotiation of meaning and compromise, and a process whose success is defined by the extent to which the new enterprise is jointly owned.

## REFERENCE

Bridges, W. and Mitchell, S. (2002) 'Leading transition: A new model for change' in Hesselbein, F. and Johnston, R. (eds.) *On leading change: A leader to leader guide.* San Francisco: Jossey-Bass, 33–46.

---

### Interrogating practice

1   What long-term transitioning projects have you been, or might you be, involved in delivering?
2   With new initiatives like the **TEF** coming along, how might these best be led? Are there particular ideas from this case study that have helped your thinking?

Implicit in Case study 9.1 is an approach developed in the US in the last century called **appreciative inquiry (AI)**. Unlike problem solving, AI seeks to develop fresh and creative thinking, focusing on future action. At its core is a series of dialogues which seek out the positive narratives upon which to build the future. **AI** can, at its most simple, be summed up as the 4 Ds:

- Discovery: finding what is working well
- Dream: envisaging what might be
- Design: engaging in dialogue to plan for the future
- Deployment: implementing the proposed design.

Rather than being a deficit model approach, this is a much more appreciative. It is a creative process which seeks out existing best practice, builds on this and then determines how to embed further innovation.

## *Growing from the ground: the snowball approach*

This approach pilots a new initiative with the people who are best placed to understand the change proposed, accept it at both a cognitive and affective level, and commit to making it work. There are various tools and techniques which can assist with the mapping of where any particular department or group of staff might be based in terms of their past history of transitioning. One useful model 'appreciates' where staff are in terms of their emotions: the **Kübler-Ross Transition Curve**.

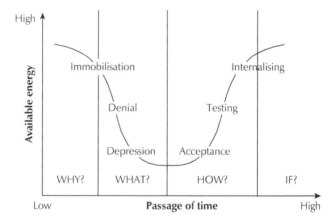

**Figure 9.1** The Kübler-Ross Transition Curve

Adapted from Kübler-Ross (1969)

In determining the readiness of individuals, or teams, to move through change, the Transition Curve (Kübler-Ross 1969) has proved immensely helpful to many organisations at the corporate, team and individual level.

As an introduction to this model, originally developed to aid those suffering from bereavement, Kübler-Ross argues that any change represents a loss to the individual undergoing the change. Thus, to bring about effective transitioning, leaders need to assist individuals to move through this curve, helping them climb back up the right-hand side, so as to regain their confidence and self-esteem, with embedded new understandings and behaviours. The skill and insight required here of leaders is to:

- recognise that different people move through this curve at different speeds, with some individuals dropping back down to the bottom of the curve if they are not properly supported;
- decide an appropriate recalibration period (with continued support) that is both fair and realistic;
- consider at what point in time individuals should be expected to move on without support, having made the transition to the shared vision.

Moving on to Case study 9.2, readers will note that 'snowball' transitioning is undertaken only with those sections of the university capable of moving rapidly through the transition curve, thereby offering an example of what success looks like to others. Observing and talking to colleagues who have embraced the requisite skills and behaviours assists observers to let go and undertake the transition themselves. The transition highlighted in the case study which follows started from the premise that the university's culture needed to be a key determinant in the conceptualisation and planning of any transformational change. Gilly Salmon, introducing a major cross-university initiative, therefore deployed the **snowball approach**, and saw a steady and sustained increase in confidence across the university as a result.

Her approach was to initially work with small integrated teams of academics, learning technologists and information specialists in practical workshops. The snowball approach occurred after participants returned to their departments and faculties, reporting on the usefulness of the workshops and encouraging others to attend. Once this approach had gained traction, the whole exercise was scaled up and extended to the full range of staff engaged in the student learning experience. The workshops subsequently became entirely digital and flexible. Gilly Salmon, recently appointed pro-vice-chancellor of education innovation at the University of Western Australia, writes about her approach when VP at Swinburne.

## Case study 9.2: Seizing the day at Swinburne University of Technology, Melbourne, Australia

### Gilly Salmon, University of Western Australia

**Organisational culture** means shared values, norms of behaviour and relationships at work . . . in other words how people relate to and support developments. In twenty-first-century universities, such relationships and influences include the whole range of ways of achieving change – whether change is even possible and whether it has a constructive impact. Probably one of the most pressing and contested areas is achieving innovations associated with exploiting new technologies for academic practice. Enabling academic staff to constructively and rapidly adopt forward-looking learning and teaching processes is pressing. Any change processes – and many have been tried and failed – must essentially take account of a multitude of embedded cultures which can be enabling, but also powerful barriers.

At Swinburne University of Technology a number of principles were adopted to promote a forward-looking, enabling culture. We believed that creating a sense of urgency was a critical factor in achieving change. The usual approaches were deliberately 'disrupted', including closing a well-rehearsed set of professional development activities. We adopted highly practical workshops called **Carpe Diem** enabling each course leader to design new teaching and learning processes, based on students' learning outcomes. Small teams, which included learning technologists and information specialists, were set up to help them and were involved as peers from the very beginning of the design events. Our research showed that colleagues' attitudes and beliefs about what is possible began to change quite quickly, when they were taking part, and they thought that they could achieve worthwhile changes in their teaching quickly and effectively. Many returned to their faculties and departments, and encouraged their peers to attend too.

We then decided to scale up the **Carpe Diem** workshops by creating one mass workshop that would include twenty course teams. The academic teams, the professionals involved (typically librarians, technologists, student services) and students themselves quickly became committed to each other's achievements and offered constructive feedback and support. We sought to constantly improve the workshop experience and ensure that the very latest pedagogical evidence and digital technologies were available, through setting up a research observatory and by encouraging the **Carpe Diem** designers to evaluate their new-style courses. We began to see the real beginnings of change in relationships – the start of a **culture change** in front of our eyes, and one that proved sustainable.

Postscript: This change has sustained since I have left Swinburne and I am now using the same approach to transform the teaching at a large research-intensive university – it is going incredibly well.

For further details see http://www.gillysalmon.com/journal-articles.html.

---

## Interrogating practice

1 What are the advantages and disadvantages of using the 'growing from the ground' (the **snowball approach**) over the 'led from the top' approach?
2 How successful have your institution's programmes been in improving the digital literacy skills of staff? What has worked well? What not so well? Could this ongoing process be done better? If so, how?

The approach used in Case study 9.2 is one which many would suggest depends on having a good sense of where best to pilot initiatives to ensure successful outcomes. Different institutions will have different sets of criteria or statistics which help them judge a school's or department's ability to be at the forefront of academic developments (e.g. teaching module feedback, graduate employment, number of staff qualified to teach). One of the ways to consider the culture and sub-cultures of an organisation is to use the **cultural framework** of Figure 9.2., noting that the one area that should provide the common ground is 'shared values'. If this is not the case, then much foundation work will need to be undertaken.

The cultural anatomy model is interesting in terms of assessing where an organisation is in terms of its readiness for change – with both its 'hard' measures (strategy, structure, systems) and 'soft' measures' (staff, style and skills), with shared values at the centre. In all three case studies offered in this chapter, the shared value that all staff agreed on was the need to ensure that their university was able to offer the best possible learning experience for their students. Readers will recognise this as being the 'shared value' that binds all staff as their collective goal.

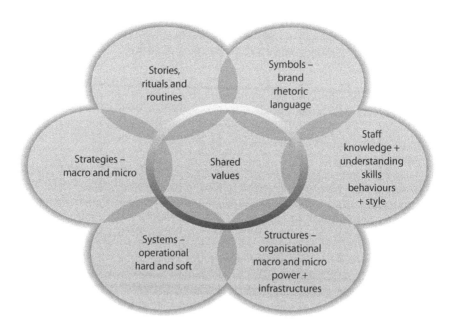

**Figure 9.2** Cultural anatomy model

Adapted from Marshall's (2007) 7s framework

## THE INCENTIVISED'APPROACH – OBTAINING THE BUY-IN FROM STAFF AND STUDENTS

The next case study, outlining a $1 billion (AUS) campus redevelopment project led by the Vice President of the University of Technology Sydney (UTS), highlights an approach where there is a clear vision, a clear timeline, a clear deadline and detailed **stakeholder mapping**.

**Stakeholder mapping** explores where different stakeholders sit on a 'power' versus 'level of interest' matrix.

In terms of high power and level of interest, students clearly populate this upper right-hand quadrant in terms of the 'power of the purse', which results from HE operating in a market economy, with student learning spaces being highly important in perceptions of attractiveness or otherwise of the university offer. With the introduction of the **Teaching Excellence Framework (TEF)** presaging higher fees in England, this will become even more crucial in the future. Other key players here are the **board** (see Chapter 3), estates, information

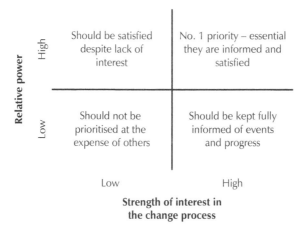

**Figure 9.3** Stakeholder mapping

systems, finance and the local community; they all have an important role to play in delivering the vision.

The change project at University of Technology, Sydney (UTS) adopted the title 'Learning2014' as the goal was to complete the major estates developments in time for the 2014 recruits. To achieve the aim, a number of incentives were proffered:

- a VC Learning2014 grant to individuals;
- annual teaching and learning awards with a category for Learning2014 implementation;
- inclusion of Learning 2014 implementation in criteria for promotion.

This major transformative project is outlined by its architect, Professor Shirley Alexander.

## Case study 9.3: A view from the top – drivers and change

### Shirley Alexander, University of Technology, Sydney

The University of Technology in Sydney (UTS) is an inner city university with 37,000 students. In 2008 it underwent a $1 billion (AUS) campus redevelopment, and at the same time we repurposed a new vision for the future of learning and teaching at UTS.

I conceived a framework for this visioning exercise as follows:

- Students – what are the contemporary needs of our students?
- Curriculum – what and how should students learn?
- Technology – given the needs of students, and this curriculum, which technologies will support our aims?
- Learning spaces – given these students, this curriculum, and these technologies, what range of learning spaces is needed?

My own conversations with students about their frustration with the lack of informal learning spaces was confirmed by the results of our annual student satisfaction survey. So we gave high priority to establishing such spaces for students.

The changing needs of students was also revealed in a national longitudinal study of first year students (James 2009). An increasing number of students are in paid work, and therefore spend less time on campus. So part of the vision emerging for the future of learning was that students should be able to have a combination of high-quality online and face-to-face experiences.

Working parties were established for each of the *future curriculum*, *technologies* and *learning spaces* components.

### Future curriculum

The committee reviewing the curriculum drew upon the new **UTS Model of Learning** which states that students should:

1 have an integrated exposure to professional practice through dynamic and multifaceted modes of *practice-oriented education*;
2 experience professional practice situated in a *global* workplace, with international mobility and international and cultural engagement as a centre piece;
3 learning opportunities which are *research-inspired* and integrated, providing academic rigour with cutting-edge technology to equip them for lifelong learning.

This committee further articulated the kinds of learning experiences students would need to have in order to achieve the aims of the model, such as work-based learning, simulation, problem-based approaches, and guest lectures by professionals in the field.

### Technologies

Examples of technologies recommended by this group (and subsequently actioned) are:

- an ePortfolio tool to document work-based learning and internships;
- support for and use of Re:View – software to support assessment of graduate attributes;
- support for and use of SparkPlus – software to support self and **peer review** of groupwork.

*Learning spaces*

A learning spaces group, which included both academic and support staff, reviewed the design of learning spaces to support changes to the design of the curriculum and the range of technologies.

One of the most critical (and controversial) decisions made was that there were to be no new standard lecture theatres constructed in the new buildings. Instead, a number of large collaborative theatres were constructed – purpose designed to facilitate in-class groupwork.

**Implementation**

The changes described above are significant, and I coined the term 'Learning2014' as the name of the project to drive them.

The Learning2014 strategy (to be renamed learning.futures from 2015 for obvious reasons) included:

- information provision;
  - videos[1] and animations[2] on what Learning2014 is
  - case studies[3] of early implementations
  - Learning2014 series (weekly seminars on related issues and technologies).
- opportunities to try out new approaches;
  - vice-chancellor's Learning2014 grants for individuals
  - communities of practice – e.g. flipped learning, use of open educational resources.
- recognition and reward;
  - annual teaching and learning awards – category for Learning2014 implementation
  - inclusion of Learning2014 implementation in criteria for promotion.

**Conclusion**

This project represents a bold new vision for the future of HE and a systematic approach to reinventing learning. A whole campus has been constructed to facilitate this vision. Critical to its success will be our ability to provide the highly engaging, inter-active learning experiences that will make it worthwhile for our students to attend campus, and to develop the depth and range of skills needed for future employment.

## NOTES

1 *What is Learning2014?* https://www.youtube.com/watch?v=rL0eFmac7mA
2 *Learning2014 explained to potential students* https://www.youtube.com/watch?v=E6db8lY7rJY
3 http://www.uts.edu.au/research-and-teaching/teaching-and-learning/learning-futures/new-approaches/case-studies

## REFERENCES

James, R., Krause, K.L. and Jennings, C. (2009) *The first year experience in Australian universities: Lessons from 1994 to 2009.*
Learning2014, http://www.uts.edu.au/research-and-teaching/teaching-and-learning/learningfutures/overview (accessed 16 August 2015).
Re:View, https://www.review-edu.com/ (accessed 16 August 2015).
SparkPlus, http://spark.uts.edu.au/ (accessed 16 August 2015).

---

### Interrogating practice

1 How does your institution involve students in planning, implementation and transitioning?
2 Consider the approach used in the case study above. How does it resonate with approaches used in your institution? Are there any techniques suggested here that you might wish to consider? If so, which?

Case study 9.3 not only illustrates the incentivising approach, but also ties together the various strands of this chapter in that it highlights a bold, audacious vision for the university, to be delivered over six years, identifying its component parts and determining key milestones. It demonstrates some very astute **stakeholder mapping**, including determining appropriate incentives to get the buy-in required to make this transition a success, as opposed to the change to a new set of campus buildings.

## SUMMARY

In this chapter three frameworks for leading transitions were examined:

- leading from the top (which was a cascade down from government policy, requiring a longer term approach to be effective)
- growing from the ground (**snowball effect**, harnessing the willingness, appetite and commitment from recognised parts of the university to trial new approaches)
- incentivising approach (determining the various incentives which would get both staff and students and engaging in the process).

All three required careful consideration on the part of the VP leading the transitioning, to determine how best to get staff and students to let go of the old, whilst holding on to past practice but also appreciating the need for change practice and behaviours. Three different techniques or tools were flagged up as useful when thinking about how best to engage with and support staff in their transitiionig: **appreciative inquiry**, the **Kübler-Ross Transition Curve**, the **cultural anatomy model**, and **stakeholder mapping**. Follow-up reading on each of these is highlighted at the end of this chapter.

In summary, to lead successful transitioning, ensure you:

1 define criteria to gauge success (as in Case study 9.1's ongoing monitoring approach);
2 inspire commitment (all three case studies were led by highly committed and driven VPs);
3 provide ongoing support and resources to support staff (in all three case studies there were timely workshops, both online and face-to-face, plus dedicated financial support to ease realisation of the vision).

Planned properly, leading transitions should not be an overly daunting task but be exciting and a creative part of your role.

## FURTHER READING

Appreciative Inquiry, http://www.new-paradigm.co.uk/Appreciative.htm (accessed 14 August 2015).

Bridges, W. (2009) *Managing transitions: Making the most of change.* 3rd edn. London: Nicholas Brealey.

A really useful and well-respected guide to dealing with the human and emotional side of organisational change, which incorporates the Kübler-Ross approach of how to manage the different stages of celebrating key aspects of the past that will feature in the future (e.g. the **appreciative inquiry** approach), letting go and moving into the new normal. Incorporating many illustrative models, this book provides a great constructive tool to assist in the planning of change.

Marshall, S. (ed.) (2007) *Strategic leadership of change in HE: What's new?* London: Routledge.

Further to the previous chapter, sections of this book (most particularly chapter 1) explore techniques such as **stakeholder mapping** and the **cultural anatomy model**. Readers should find chapter 1, 'Leading and managing strategic change', particularly useful in that it provides much more detail about the whole change process, including a range of incentives for staff to become engaged in transitions. It also contains twelve UK case studies of pan-university change led by members of the senior team.

## REFERENCES

Bridges, W. (2009) *Managing transitions: Making the most of change.* 3rd edn. London: Nicholas Brealey.
Kübler-Ross, E. (1969) *On death and dying.* London: Routledge.
Marshall, S. (ed.) (2007) *Strategic leadership of change in HE: What's new?* London: Routledge.

# Part IV
# Looking to the future

# 10: Future scenarios

## Looking to think 'outside in'

## OVERVIEW

It would be easy if we were able to gaze into a crystal ball and see a clear vision of what higher education (HE) will look like in, say, 2050. Increasingly, the development of university corporate strategies commences with such crystal ball gazing, resulting in some significantly long-term approaches such as the UCL 2015–2034 Strategic Plan. In other universities, a ten-year horizon is as far as leaders can reasonably forecast. Whichever horizon they focus upon, there are a number of publications that are assisting the shaping of perspectives (see IPPR, 2013; PA Consulting, 2014). Among the regularly rehearsed challenges in terms of futureproofing are six core concerns and these are highlighted in Table 10.1.

With such a range of challenges and uncertainties, no wonder that the current model of HE is being brought into question. So, how do HE leaders make sense of the above, whether in established higher education institutions (HEIs) or those who are entering as new providers. The recent PA Consulting annual survey of Higher Education in the UK (2014) reported that 92 per cent of vice-chancellors were confident in the long-term resilience of their own HEI (the survey had a 1/3 response rate). Meanwhile, a year earlier, IPPR (2013) was predicting that 'an avalanche is coming', suggesting complacency amongst HE leaders, and stating (pp. 4–5) that:

> Just as **globalisation** and technology have transformed other huge sectors of the economy in the past 20 years, in the next 20 years universities face transformation . . . Deep, radical and urgent transformation is required in higher education. The biggest risk is that as

a result of complacency, caution or anxiety, the pace of change is too slow and the nature of change is too incremental. The models of higher education that marched triumphantly across the globe in the second half of the 20th century are broken . . . Leaders will need to have a keen eye towards creating value for their students.

Against this uncertain future, the key concern of this chapter is how leaders create value for their students. It will focus on three particular areas: firstly, greater use of technology to enhance student learning; secondly, exploring new models of tertiary education, to include,

**Table 10.1** Six core future-proofing concerns

| | |
|---|---|
| Rapidly changing technological innovations | • increased use of blended learning<br>• learning design informed by analytics<br>• augmented learning and dynamic assessment<br>• greater significance of tracking metrics including learning gain<br>• MOOCs |
| Market forces operating within part of a rapidly growing global market | • borderless education<br>• internationalised curricula to suit an increasingly golbalised market<br>• growth of transnational education<br>• changing demographics to include exponential scaling up of the Indian and Chinese student population<br>• new tertiary education providers |
| Reimagined learning spaces | • virtual or cyber<br>• revitalisation of estates and innovations in the architectural environment<br>• transformation of libraries into 'learning commons'<br>• growth of simulated learning labs |
| Growth of interdisciplinarity and notions of lifelong learning | • curriculum overhaul<br>• cross-discipline module exploration of global 'wicked issues'<br>• earning whilst learning |
| Changing student expectations | • more student-centred learning approaches<br>• personalised learning accounts<br>• greater use of appropriate social media<br>• $24 \times 7$ opportunities to engage with learning |
| Changing employer expectations | • requirement for graduates to be able to hit the ground running<br>• higher-order level of skills required (technical, behavioural and critical thinking) |

where appropriate, seamless pathways into HE; and, finally, an **unbundled** and **rebundled** approach to the future (determining what is valued by students and continues to add value to the student learning experience, *then* introducing an enhanced offer in response to global trends). Each is considered below, with case study contributors coming from outwith the traditional HE sector, offering their distinct views. Interestingly, the creative project ideas they offer are not so unthinkable to progressive leaders of teaching and learning: such approaches are already either in embryonic form or being deployed to good effect.

## TECHNOLOGICAL ADVANCES TO ENHANCE STUDENT LEARNING

The IPPR report referred to earlier was a sharp reminder (if not a wake-up call) to leaders in HE to the fact that the technological change and innovation already underway had the potential to be seriously disruptive. A significant number of university staff have been slow to keep up with digital developments, particularly in the social media space. Further to the introduction of **MOOCs**, which grew out of the **Khan Academy** in the US, many HE providers initially refused to recognise the potential of **MOOCs** beyond branding. Meanwhile, others started to using them creatively, for example to supplement standard programmes, as illustrated in the University of Miami's online high school, designed to assist prospective students to achieve well in the biology component of their Scholastic Aptitude Tests (SATs). This trend is now well underway in the UK, with **FutureLearn** run by the Open University (www.futurelearn.com) in its third year, alongside **Udacity**, **Coursera** and **edX** offers. All have grown to be increasingly creative in their offer and deployment.

As the use of virtual learning spaces in HE has become more sophisticated, so has the blend of learning approaches such as online chat rooms and access to a range of online course materials. Alongside these developments has been the growth and use of **learning analytics**, with learning technicians able to monitor students' progress, and provide forward feedback (e.g. 'if you carry on as you are, you are moving towards achievement of . . . ' or 'however, if you aspire to higher marks, you will need to . . . '). These provide a clear focus for both student and tutor dialogue. Another trend that Pearson is predicting is much greater use of such personalised learning, as outlined in the case study below.

## Case study 10.1: Let's get personal

**Stephen Gomez, Pearson Education**

Predicting the future can be a perilous occupation, not least because the very act of uttering the prediction mysteriously seems to negate it! However, we think we can be confident in our particular prediction as it is based on the inexorable trend of increasing numbers of learners entering HE. Universities are responding to this dramatic increase and are looking towards new technologies, particularly communication tools for solutions. Widening access attracts a greater diversity of learners with a broad range of previous knowledge, abilities and learning styles. This can bring vibrancy to the learning experience but can also mean some students struggle with a more traditional model – decreasing student satisfaction and affecting student retention, progression and transition. So, how can we cope with large numbers of diverse learners within a one-size-fits-all mass education system?

In 2025 we see the lecture as the central spine of a student's learning experience, but these **lifestyle lectures** are very different from those we know today. Our prediction is in a new model of personalised lecture where the pathway, access and support have been designed for the student to tailor their learning experience. Students will be encouraged to think about the way they learn, their lifestyle and commitments, building a personalised package that supports their learning pathway. Already students can select modules and timetables but this additional flexibility means students away from campus can dial-in remotely from across the world or attend a local connected hub. This would encourage a truly globalised experience for learners with participants learning in many countries together, working on common curriculum but in a bespoke way.

Students' lecture-learning will be supported by a new generation of commercially available digital learning resources. Within the education publishing world, there is a quiet revolution taking place as products are moving inexorably from the printed textbook to online resources. By 2025, the range and, more importantly, the sophistication of learning resources available for students and their tutors will be extensive. Digital resources will move from the current **eText** versions of the printed word to highly immersive and engaging multimedia experiences. **Learner analytics** available from these resources has the potential to boost learning. For the learner, individual pathways will be charted through these new resources based on the individual learner's own performance. Opportunities to self-assess their understanding and receive immediate feedback and communicate and share with peers throughout the world will be standard. For tutors, knowledge of the performance of their students whilst they are teaching rather than just at the end of their teaching block will allow better targeting of learning support for those students who require more assistance. For publishers, the data will help establish the efficacy of their resources and help provide evidence to drive a learning sciences approach to understanding how learners interact and engage with digital resources so that they can improve engagement and motivation of students to eventually drive better student performance.

Looking at the vision for 2025 we can see that a mass education system can begin to meet individual needs. With learning technologies and communication tools and a bit of creativity, there is a real opportunity to truly deliver a personal, but potentially global, student experience.

---

### Interrogating practice

1. What form of **learning analytics** does your institution use? Is ongoing forward feedback part of the monitoring?
2. How regular is your institution's feedback to students? Is it providing the rigorous and robust feedback that informs their academic achievement?

As HE providers seek to extend their reach, approaches such as those illustrated in Case study 10.1 clearly provide a ready opportunity to operate globally, and to provide bespoke packaging whether it be for individuals or groups. Consideration of ways of integrating these with the 'learn as you earn' approach is already underway. Indeed, since crystal ball gazers are predicting the growth of tertiary education more generally, **apprenticeships** – such as those operated in the

UK – provide a package much more suitable to those learners wishing to engage in continuous upskilling whilst learning. Case study 10.2, written by Anne Morrison, notes the real value of apprenticeships in her role at the BBC. She predicts that the future will see even greater deployment of this form of tertiary education, thereby satisfying the needs of both the learners and the companies that employ them as apprentices.

## Case study 10.2: The rise of Higher Apprenticeships

### Anne Morrison, formerly of the BBC

Today's students are entering a world in which a job for life has disappeared and even long-term employment is unlikely: a fast-changing world where they are going to have to keep pitching themselves and their skills for new work, where the skills that are required are themselves changing and where the jobs they will be doing in five or ten years' time may not have even been invented yet.

So employability is not just about the first job you get out of university. It is about how to get the fourth or fifth job: how to sustain yourself in work throughout your career.

Universities tend to reward individual effort whereas when students get to the world of work, as employers we are looking for their ability to collaborate and work well in a team, their communication and presentation skills, their drive and self-awareness. In the fast changing world of the future, adaptability and flexibility will be key, as will resilience and the ability to keep on learning. Sometimes these are called 'soft skills', a slightly pejorative term given that they are quite hard to find.

Increasingly universities need to educate the whole person, ensuring that useful extracurricular activities do not get squeezed out by an exclusive emphasis on academic work. Students studying a course as a way in to a particular industry, often taking on debt to do so, have a right to expect it to deliver on its promise to be industry-relevant. This is best achieved through partnerships between employers and HE so that graduates are able to bridge the gap between the two worlds. This can take many forms: work experience, industry accreditation, practitioners in residence, industry case studies, guest lectures and joint research projects. In a more radical form, this partnership can affect the shape of the degree itself.

Take the example of the BBC's Technology Apprenticeships, which began when I was Director of the BBC Academy. These are innovative Higher Apprenticeships leading to a Bachelor of Engineering (B. Eng) degree after three years. They were originally co-funded by BBC Engineering and the **Department for Business, Innovation and Skills's (BIS)** Employer Ownership Fund and were set up to address the industry-wide problem of an aging demographic in broadcasting engineering and technology. They arose out of a partnership between the industry, Birmingham City and Salford Universities, and **Creative Skillset**. We set up an industry wide employer group overseeing the strategy and skills and created the B. Eng from scratch based on industry needs, which were then played back to the universities. The apprentices are BBC staff on three-year contracts. In that time the academic syllabus is taught by Salford and Birmingham City universities while the BBC Academy draws on BBC expertise to teach practical skills to apply that new knowledge to the practice of broadcast engineering. The apprentices also have work placements with engineering teams in the BBC and selected industry partners such as ITV and Arqiva. There are major benefits to the apprentices, who receive a salary rather than paying £9,000 annual tuition fees and who end up with an industry-relevant degree with excellent employment prospects. Employers benefit by achieving greater diversity in the workforce and filling skills gaps. The universities benefit by having the opportunity to develop new work-based learning models for undergraduates. They may be able to schedule tuition to fill in downtime and monetise their facilities. The model appears to be a successful one for all sides, which could have a wider application to other areas. This is what I see as the future.

---

## Interrogating practice

1   How are your students assisted in bridging the gap between HE and the world of work? How strategic is your approach?
2   How do your students gain 'soft skills'? Is this part of your **Graduate Attributes** Framework? How are these measured?

The approach illustrated in Case study 10.2 sits well with the vision of a number of universities as they have seen new pathways into higher education further to growth in terms of their tertiary education provision. For example, the University of Salford is well known for its Media City, which is based on the model highlighted above. The university proposes to take the idea further in its new vision of creating 'industrial learning zones'. Within these learning zones, both students and industrialists will work together on real-time projects. Other universities are developing similar sorts of shared space environments for real-time learning, which has implications for investment in and development of the estate. The added advantage of a really clear, focused and distinctive approach is a greater value proposition for students. So, in thinking about how to future proof one's offer, determining appropriate learning spaces is an all important consideration.

## UNBUNDLING AND REBUNDLING HIGHER EDUCATION

Sue Littlemore, offering a journalist's perspective, is adamant that considerations of what distinctive space an existing (HEI) wants to inhabit will indeed inform the future of HE, but may not cause the tectonic shifts that some forecasters have predicted. Littlemore offers a view which suggests that, whilst there will be some unbundling of the offer, it may be **rebundled** as it was before, subject to certain updating.

### Case study 10.3: Look outside and see what's coming down the line

**Sue Littlemore, former BBC Education Correspondent**

A speaker asked an audience of university leaders, 'How many vice-chancellors does it take to change a light bulb?'

Almost as one, the members of the audience frowned and replied, 'Change?'

It is a bit of an old gag – I have heard (and told) various versions a few times – but it reflects the HE sector's reputation for not being good at change.

That's not to say universities today are the same as a decade ago – they can now charge higher student fees, for example.

It is true, though, that the sector can appear to be one which tends to get changed by others, rather than confidently looking ahead and outside of itself to come up with its own innovations.

That is the challenge for the next generation of university leaders.

To date, most universities have pursued more or less the same core aims: recruit more school leavers and foreign students; rise up the league tables, especially in research; enhance the student experience, etc.

These should not necessarily be discarded, but over the next decade there will be a number of external pressures that bold and forward thinking university leaders might anticipate and use to drive sector-wide or institution-level reforms.

Graduate debt, for example. People who are studying for their degrees now will be living with the impact of paying back their £27,000 maximum tuition fee in 2025.

According to the Sutton Trust, higher and middle earners will be paying their fees back into their forties and fifties. A middle-aged teacher, the Trust reports, might have to find an extra £2,500 a year.

Once the burden of graduate debt is felt, vice-chancellors will be under greater pressure to demonstrate families are getting value for money. I say families, because many parents are now heavily involved in the funding and the choosing of which university. Parents are HE 'customers' as much as students.

A wise university leader will pay great attention to that and signs that public opinion is increasingly sceptical about what universities deliver.

The majority of parents with children in secondary school (60 per cent) do not think university degrees are worth the money. That was the finding of a **YouGov/Guardian poll**, published in 2014, which sampled 11,000 parents of eleven- to seventeen-year-olds from all social backgrounds across England and Wales. This attitude did not vary between affluent and less well-off parents.

Research from the consumer organisation **Which?** echoes that warning. It concluded that while the majority of students say they are satisfied with their course, one-third of students disagree their course is good value.

**Which?** has suggested improvements to the quality and transparency of information applicants receive. But here is an opportunity for vice-chancellors to snatch the lead, and make the change themselves.

Twin demands from employers, for the graduates they want; and from graduates, for the jobs they want, will continue to pressurise universities. It is also another chance to grasp the agenda.

This is an area where many new private providers hope to build their reputations. Other parts of the sector should not want to be left behind. There is a good opportunity for university leaders to come up with their own fresh and successful ways of working together with employers and graduates.

In ten years an excellent UK HE sector should still be doing what it does well today. And more.

Ideally it will have looked outside itself, anticipated new expectations and designed its own reforms.

A danger to be avoided is that by 2025 our universities will not have driven much change at all.

## REFERENCES

Crawford, C. and Wenchao, J. (2014) 'Payback time: Student debt and loan repayments: What will the 2012 reforms mean for graduates?' *The Sutton Trust* 10 April 2014. Available from http://www.suttontrust.com/researcharchive/payback-time/ (accessed 16 September 2015).

The Sutton Trust (2014) 'Graduates paying off student loans into their 50s – IFS/Sutton Trust.' *The Sutton Trust* 10 April 2014. Available from http://www.suttontrust.com/newsarchive/graduates-paying-student-loans-50s-ifssutton-trust/ (accessed 16 September 2015).

Which? (2014) *A degree of value: Value for money from the student perspective.* Available from http://www.staticwhich.co.uk/documents/pdf/a-degree-of-value-value-for-money-from-the-student-perspective-which-report-386517.pdf (accessed 16 September 2015).

YouGov (2014) 'Parents think university too expensive, but necessary.' *YouGov* 26 February 2014. Available from https://yougov.co.uk/news/2014/02/26/parents-think-university-too-expensive-necessary/ (accessed 16 September 2015).

In short, Littlemore is proposing that university leaders should 'snatch the lead' to fend off the many new providers who are entering the market with no history or traditions holding them back. This is the key consideration of the next chapter, which will go through a range of suggestions as to just how leaders develop themselves and their institution's offer so as to be agile and flexible enough to snatch a lead and meet the challenges of the future.

## SUMMARY

This chapter explored the range of changes that are in evidence today as well as speculating about the changes we might see in the future. It deals with some crucial challenges, reconciling mass HE with personalisation through technology, combining the individual learning expectations of students with the higher skills required in the workplace, and the revisiting of the **psychological contract** between universities, students and employers by looking from outside in.

In terms of consensus, six key challenges were identified: technological changes, market forces, learning spaces, interdisciplinary learning for life, student expectations, and employer expectations. There will not be a single HE provider who is not concerned to keep on top, if not ahead, of all six However, three of these challenges present great uncertainties, for example, technological changes. Not only do students themselves expect to be using the latest technologies, as represented in the **virtual learning environments (VLE)** and component parts, they will be expected to use them. Such capabilities enhance a provider's ability to analyse student learning, give ongoing feedback as to where the learner's strengths are, support them where developmental areas have been identified, and seek to assist students realise their potential.

The second area of challenge is that posed as a result of the global recognition that a country's economic development will not be achieved without the workforce acquiring a core higher skillset. The innovation which is happening at speed globally – particularly in the Far East – is that of tertiary education. The apprenticeship model that has emerged in recent years in the UK offers a means to address the increasing higher level skills shortage and is required to rebalance the emphasis on the knowledge economy.

Finally, this chapter explored the need for universities to have a long-term vision of the unique and distinctive value proposition they are offering their students. There is a strong case for **unbundling** or deconstructing the current offer, though, as Littlemore argues, it could be a case of **rebundling** existing aspects of the offer, to ensure that it is fit for purpose. The **unbundling** may reveal the need to seek alternative learning spaces, or introduce more inter-disciplinarity to give graduates the edge in looking to their futures. Whatever the future holds it is crucial that leaders understand how best to lead through this complex landscape, determining their own unique and distinctive learning environment.

## FURTHER READING

IPPR (2013) *A critical path: Securing the future of higher education in England*. London: IPPR. Available from www.ippr.org/publications/a-critical-path-securing-the-future-of-higher-education-in-england (accessed 12 July 2015).

IPPR provide a number of useful reports on considering the future of HE, and this is no exception. In this report they set out how the UK can continue to expand and reform HE whilst being mindful of the drive for austerity, and protecting teaching and research. They argue that this is essential if the sector is to be equipped to play a leading role in economic and social renewal in the future. A good provocative read.

PA Consulting (2015) *Lagging behind: Are UK universities falling behind in the global innovation race?* Available from www.paconsulting.com/our-thinking/higher-education-report-2015 (accessed 12 July 2015).

PA Consulting provide some useful overview surveys and reports that are always good for stimulating thinking. Their most recent HE report suggests that globally, university education is facing unprecedented pressure for reform from multiple perspectives. Growth in student numbers alongside consumerist attitudes has led to demands for more flexible and cheaper study options. New technologies continue to challenge traditional teaching models. And finally, new providers are bringing about a game-changing landscape. This publication explores this landscape.

## REFERENCES

PA Consulting (2014) *Here be dragons.* Available from www.paconsulting. com/our-thinking/higher-education-report-2014 (accessed 17 August 2015).

Rizvi, S., Donnelly, K. and Barber, M. (2013) *An avalanche is coming: HE and the revolution ahead.* London: IPPR. Available from http://www.ippr. org/publications/an-avalanche-is-coming-higher-education-and-the-revolution-ahead (accessed 8 July 2015).

UCL 2015–2034 Strategic Plan. Available from www.ucl.ac.uk/ucl-2034 (accessed 21 August 2015).

# 11: Leading teaching and learning

## What does the future hold?

## OVERVIEW

So, given all the analysis, thoughts and reflections presented in the previous chapters, what does the future really hold for leaders of teaching and learning? This book has offered a range of practical tips, techniques and narratives of best practice. Hopefully, across all the chapters, you, the reader, will have noted the lack of prescription, the lack of a list of so-called appropriate competencies, or a one-size-fits-all approach. Throughout the book, the constant theme is about role modelling, with agility, flexibility and authenticity working in harness to anticipate the future needs of our graduates. The best way to predict the future, and to ensure that the key components in which we believe passionately feature, is to shape it.

A further key message throughout this book has been 'collaboration and co-creation' – working together to shape the future, be it with staff, students or other key stakeholders. Right through to Part IV, Chapter 10, well-known individuals in the sector have offered their perspectives on just what they believe will assist in the future-proofing of their practice, to shape a rapidly changing learning landscape. This chapter, however, goes beyond their suggested approaches, to flag up three key concerns regarding leading teaching and learning. These are important challenges that have, as yet, to be fully addressed if leaders are truly serious about bringing about a transformation in the way students experience higher education (HE). The rhetoric is there, but the reality, sadly, is still lacking.

In looking to shape the future, leaders will require full and collective staff engagement and delivery, and this necessitates the design of a new paradigm for HE, which has been alluded to in this text. It is about:

- harnessing the huge potential and power of technology;
- creating something far more uplifting and inclusive than ever before;
- working collectively and in an interdisciplinary way

to prepare graduates to tackle the globe's **wicked issues**.

What are these three major challenges? Firstly, there is the issue of insufficient equality and diversity amongst staff holding leadership positions in our universities. For example, in the UK, almost half of the academic staff are female, but only 20 per cent of professors are female, and less than 15 per cent are in the top executive position (HESA). Secondly, we have the issue of globalisation, and the mantra of educating global citizens. We must come to understand what exactly 'global citizenship' means and how to pass this mantra on to our staff. If we are serious about equipping our students with the ability to operate as global citizens, how does such understanding present itself, let alone become embedded in the curriculum? Finally, there is the issue of interdisciplinarity. Much lip service is paid to the notion of educating students to become graduates capable of solving these so-called 'wicked issues' (e.g. climate change, aging populations) of the world, but how many university staff are capable of looking at an issue through a lens different from their own, particularly the alternative disciplinary lens (as Tarrach suggests in Chapter 2)? Increasingly, interdisciplinary research teams are forging ahead on global issues, but translating such approaches to the teaching domain often proves difficult, given quality assurance systems, subject benchmarks and credit accumulation frameworks. Despite some great efforts at introducing various modules which explore global issues from different viewpoints, they are rarely compulsory.

## EQUALITY AND DIVERSITY

As noted in the UK Equality Act 2010, equality is not about treating all people in the same way. It is about recognising and respecting diversity enough to adapt practice and procedure to suit everyone. Five years on, the issue of equality and diversity in the workplace, particularly in HE, still has a long way to go in terms of gender balance (let alone broader diversity), particularly representation in executive teams. Despite the number of females in HE globally now exceeding that of males (with a sixfold increase in female participation in the last forty years), the paucity of females holding senior positions (22 per cent) – particularly at the executive level (14 per cent) – remains an issue (HESA).

The dramatic increase in the number of females now participating in HE has not been matched by growth in the number progressing to senior leadership roles within the sector. Most senior academics and academic leaders are male, yet there has been a marked increase in the representation of women in particular jobs, for instance at vice-principal (VP) (Teaching and Learning) level. However, this is the level at which many hit a glass ceiling, failing to progress to the very top jobs. This is certainly the case in Australia, where 40 per cent of VPs are female, but only 18 per cent leading entire institutions. In the UK, female VPs (Teaching and Learning) bemoan the fact that they have hit a real glass ceiling, or, for some, a glass cliff in that they seem to take on a poison chalice in terms of expectations. As a result, if they don't succeed, it is often blamed on the fact that they are too soft, i.e. a woman (see Morley 2013).

Then, *in extremis*, we witness some developing nations that clearly have a long way to go. Hong Kong is one such example, with one female VP, and no female presidents. At the other extreme is Sweden, where 43 per cent of rectors/presidents are female (Morley 2013). In the case of the latter, balance has been achieved through two means: firstly, legislation that requires all public bodies to provide annual returns with gender statistics on students *and* staff at all levels and, secondly, the identification of a range of substantive career development activities.

So, how do we move forward on this pressing agenda? Moving beyond one institution, or one nation, we need a global response, flagging up and learning from good practice wherever it may reside. Analysis as well of the 'structures of inequality' (perceived and/or real) which militate against the entry of women into senior roles needs to be undertaken so as to address these. The combination of seeking out best practice and uncovering barriers to progression has led to a number of countries taking initiatives such as:

- women only leadership programmes (for example, the UK Leadership Foundation's **Aurora Programme**);
- **gender mainstreaming** (for example, promoted in the **EU Treaty of Amsterdam** 1997);

- **affirmative action** (for example, the US **ACE programme**);
- quotas and targets (for example, the UK government's target of 25 per cent of board membership to be women).

I would argue that the so-called 'female' traits of agility and flexibility, (Morley 2013) equip females well to reinvigorate the debate around appropriate leadership capabilities and future-proofing the sector. A flexible, organic values-driven pursuit of a vision rather than a strictly linear, **key performance indicator (KPI)** driven strategic approach may be more appropriate in today's world. Not that the two are incompatible: both are required in equal measure, but in an agile way!

The most influential actors in this challenge include chairs of HE councils and governing bodies (often predominantly male), executive search firms (often male-led), and human resources – both on the management and the development side. Professionals and researchers working in the field of gender equality need to focus on the simple target of an employee demographic in HE that comes closer to a mirror of the student body.

And gender is just one aspect of challenge that leaders of HE need to address if we are serious about providing graduates with the best possible teaching environment in which they see inclusivity and role modelling in action. As PricewaterhouseCoopers (2008) notes when commenting on the 'leaky pipeline of career progression':

> There is no evidence in external research or interviews that the leakage will evolve and disappear; there is, however, much evidence that positive action can help.

What might positive action look like, to start addressing this issue? There is an existing range of research on four different approaches, as outlined below:

- recognition of the issue (e.g. understanding what the statistics tell us);
- **mentoring and coaching** (e.g. what schemes are offered via HR departments to those in minority groups?);
- **shadowing** opportunities (e.g. are staff provided with opportunities to work alongside those in more senior positions, to consider what their further development needs might be?);
- targets (e.g. the Scottish Government's introduction of gender quotas regarding membership of public boards).

---

**Interrogating practice**

1 What does the gender balance look like in your top team? What messages does this send to other staff?
2 Does your institution have policies around the four approaches outlined above?
3 What more do you think that the sector could do as a whole?

---

## GLOBALISATION AND THE DEVELOPMENT OF GLOBAL CITIZENS

**Globalisation** or, more accurately, the bringing together of different cultures and cultural exchange, can really drive leading-edge innovation. Constructive approaches combine expanding individuals' breadth and depth of knowledge and understanding, with viewing issues from different global perspectives. In a recent survey undertaken by the **HEA** and the Higher Education Policy Institute (2015), students were surveyed as to their views on their international peers; the majority believed international students enhanced their undergraduate study. However, how many academic staff maximise the opportunities to be gained from this rich mix of cultures? Universities still find it difficult to avoid **ghettoisation** of different cultures, particularly in residential accommodation. If we are serious about bringing about greater cultural understanding, how better to do this than encouraging a cultural mix of students not only to study together, but to eat together, take part in extracurricular activities together, and so on. Before suggesting how **globalisation** might play out in higher education institutions (HEIs) in the future, it is worth spending some time defining our terms.

What, exactly, is globalisation? Is it the same as internationalisation? And, if so, how does this manifest itself in terms of the curriculum, in content and pedagogic approaches. Is it a process, or is it an outcome?

In looking at graduate outcomes as defined in institutional teaching and learning strategies from across the globe, both the UK and Australia refer to 'global citizenship' (or some such equivalence) as a key **graduate attribute**. Australia identifies eight key graduate competencies, with the eighth being 'using cultural understanding' (the other seven are finding and using information, communicating, planning and organising, working with others and teams, numeracy, problem solving, and using technology). Similarly, for the UK, the Quality Assurance Agency (2007) outlines a similar list, with the ninth attribute being 'an understanding of the need for a high level of ethical, social, cultural, environmental and wider professional conduct'. How can these two countries be confident that this is a key achievable outcome? The challenge remains: what are the various component inputs which will lead to the achievement of this output, i.e. the 'global citizen' and the associated outcomes?

Internationalising the curriculum remains a major challenge – despite all the work that has taken place to assist this process over the past ten years – primarily because it remains a contested notion. Whilst recognising that inclusive curriculum content and the associated pedagogical approaches are crucial for bringing about the best learning experience for all students, it is clear that the rhetoric is much simpler than the reframing required. Internationalising the curriculum involves providing students with global perspectives of their own discipline, and exploring key issues from different cultural viewpoints. We do our students a great disservice if we do not assist them in the development of a set of values and skills to enable them to gain purposeful employment in diverse cultural environments. All this, however, is predicated on teaching staff having the necessary awareness, understanding and willingness, alongside competence, to bring about the required changes to both their approach and practice. The responsibility for this upskilling is ultimately the responsibility of the VP (Teaching and Learning). And, once again, without role modelling, i.e. being able to walk the talk, only lip service will be paid to **globalisation**, internationalisation, and the promotion of global citizenship.

## Interrogating practice

1  What demonstrable globalisation or internationalisation projects are you responsible for in your institution?
2  How successful or otherwise are these?
3  What more (if anything) could you do to ensure these themes are embedded and responsive to future developments?

In summary, **globalisation** is not just an intellectual exercise. It is about developing a propensity for action: participation – i.e. the active element of **globalisation** – has to be the key indicator of the achievement of global citizenship. This is where interdisciplinarity comes in.

## INTERDISCIPLINARITY

While disciplines form the building blocks of contemporary HE, it is increasingly recognised that students need to be prepared for a world of complex social and economic challenges, which often require multi-professional teamwork and interdisciplinary approaches. Addressing this requires the development of curriculum and pedagogy that can support students in developing skills such as critical thinking and problem solving alongside the ability to think across cultural borders. Additionally, a higher-level skill has to be the ability critically to assess one's own stance by viewing it from another discipline or individual's perspective.

Society needs capable global citizens, with an appetite to tackle the wicked issues, which require holistic approaches. But when should involvement in such problem solving begin? Ideally, such consideration would commence in compulsory schooling, (i.e. kindergarten and the subsequent twelve years) but such an approach has been driven out in certain countries with the introduction of national curricula. So, this leaves HE leaders to grasp and address this challenge.

In HE to date, interdisciplinary programmes and courses are most commonly (but not exclusively) carried out at graduate level or as a module towards the end of a degree programme. Institutional teaching and learning strategies refer to interdisciplinarity, but VPs (Teaching and Learning) are reliant on committed individuals to make it happen. Whilst the need for interdisciplinary collaboration has accelerated, there are still many systemic barriers to its introduction which work against VPs being truly successful in this area.

### Interrogating practice

1   Where does interdisciplinarity feature in your university? Is it a mainstream or voluntary activity? Does it feature in undergraduate as well as postgraduate teaching?
2   Who is responsible for leading interdisciplinarity? Is it led as part of a strategic approach?
3   Might more be done? If so, what and how?

## SUMMARY

This chapter has explored three key challenges for leaders of teaching and learning and I urge you to take up the baton with regard to them. Firstly, develop a diverse pipeline of talent, both into and beyond the role of VP (Teaching and Learning); secondly, promote and embed a truly global learning experience; and, finally, tackle the thorny issue of encouraging interdisciplinarity to equip our graduates for an interdisciplinary future.

Looking at Part IV and the last two chapters – with Chapter 10 offering challenges from three leaders working out with universities, and this, Chapter 11, giving observations from an educationist – what implications for VPs (Teaching and Learning) do each suggest? I believe the implication is that the 'old' or traditional model of HE is no longer fit for purpose. Rolling the thoughts from both chapters into my manifesto for future VPs, I came up with the following:

1   A new learning paradigm needs to be created, which takes account of a highly diverse set of learners, designed by a diverse set of staff.
2   Learning outcomes will be right at the fore, as will learning design to assist students achieve those outcomes. Learning design teams will contain a breadth of expertise to include learning technologists, librarians, student support staff, and academics.
3   A fresh, new, creative and dynamic curriculum is required, which promotes interdisciplinarity and graduate attributes such as global citizenship.
4   Learners should benefit from global and diverse cultural perspectives through being able to access a range of both virtual and real networks. Such an approach will provide much richness to a dynamic curriculum.

Leaders of teaching and learning are central to redefining outmoded models of HE and should embrace this exciting challenge. Their positive creative approach to the curriculum will be pivotal to the success of our future graduates. Their future should be just, fair, respectful of diversity and embracing difference and, above all, a positive prospect. This won't happen without HE leaders, particularly of teaching and learning, offering themselves as role models for the way ahead.

## FURTHER READING

Killick, D. (2008) *Graduate attributes for a globalized world*. York: Higher Education Academy.

Arguing that all universities should provide an education which is fit for purpose for each student, Killick suggests that fitness for purpose implies they should prepare them to live and work successfully in not only the world of today but the world of tomorrow. Aspects of this global world that need unpacking for students include the understanding and ability to influence changes in technological, economic, material, cultural, social, environmental and personal connectivity. The author also argues that to live and work successfully within this globalised world, our graduates need attributes which extend beyond the knowledge and skills traditionally delivered within a purely discipline-focused curriculum, thereby making the case for interdisciplinarity.

Morley, L. (2013) *Women and higher education leadership: Absences and aspirations*. London: Leadership Foundation for Higher Education.

This is a most comprehensive overview of the challenges facing women seeking leadership positions. It explores gendered divisions of labour in universities, gendered biases, and notions of management and masculinity that can prove difficult to break down. It does, however, also offer some global exemplars illustrating that the issue is not insurmountable: a good starting point to assist in determining national, regional and local strategies for moving forward on this agenda.

University of Edinburgh (2015) *Interdisciplinarity provision in higher education: Current context and future challenges*. York: Higher Education Academy.

This publication recognises that the need for interdisciplinary research to address global, societal challenges is accelerating. Policymakers and non-governmental organisations frequently call for an evidence base that integrates social, cultural and economic dimensions with the natural and medical sciences.

This research provides a literature review of interdisciplinary provision, maps the scale and type of current provision within the UK and looks to identify plans and trends for the future. It seeks to answer the following questions:

What are the pedagogies that are likely to provide distinctive opportunities for interdisciplinarity?

What are the key elements of effective practice that are identified within the literature?

For which of these is there a robust evidence base evaluating the effectiveness of interdisciplinarity?

What gaps exist in the existing literature in relation to: (a) types of disciplines that are not widely evaluated and for which there is a strong prima facie case that they are high impact; (b) the scope for the existing evidence bases to be further strengthened and developed?

What are the principles supporting interdisciplinarity in undergraduate and postgraduate taught education?

See more at: https://www.heacademy.ac.uk/resource/interdisciplinary-provision-higher-education-current-and-future-challenges#sthash.zWrQf9Ap.dpuf

## REFERENCES

Higher Education Policy Institute and Higher Education Academy (2015) *2015 Academic Experience Survey.* Oxford: Higher Education Policy Institute. Available from www.hepi.ac.uk/2015/06/04/2015-academic-experience-survey (accessed 10 August 2015).

Higher Education Statistics Agency (HESA) Available from www.hesa.ac.uk/stats-staff (accessed 17 August 2015).

Morley, L. (2013) *Women and higher education leadership: Absences and aspirations.* London: Leadership Foundation for Higher Education.

PricewaterhouseCoopers (2008) *The leaking pipeline: Where are our female leaders?* Available from https://www.pwc.com/en_GX/gx/women-at-pwc/assets/leaking_pipeline.pdf (accessed 15 August 2015).

Quality Assurance Agency (QAA) (2007) *Research-teaching linkages: Enhancing graduate attributes.* Available from http://www.enhancementthemes.ac.uk/docs/publications/enhancing-graduate-attributes-creative-and-cultural-practice.pdf (accessed 24 August 2015).

UK Equality Act 2010. Available from http://www.legislation.gov.uk/ukpga/2010/15/contents (accessed 14 August 2015).

# Postscript

Basing public policy on personal anecdotes is of limited value. Nonetheless, one reason I care so deeply about higher education (HE) policy and the need for stronger incentives for good university teaching is the mixed academic experience I had as an undergraduate.

It was not the university's fault. The funding for teaching each undergraduate (the 'unit-of-resource') had been falling for fifteen years when I enrolled in 1990. It was not the fault of the lecturers either, for they worked in an environment where it was nearly impossible to facilitate a personal learning experience.

The unit-of-resource went on falling for almost another decade after 1990. It took policymakers aeons to catch up. But when they did, they did so properly.[1] The key moment was the introduction of £3,000 fees backed by income-contingent loans in the Higher Education Act (2004).[2]

In 2012 the Coalition repeated Tony Blair's trick of tripling fees in the face of tough parliamentary opposition. Whatever the controversies – over the level of debt, over non-repayment rates and over the supposed marketisation of HE – universities were ensured a decent income for teaching.

I worked on those 2012 changes and still see the funding system for full-time undergraduates as broadly right. But we did try to have our cake and eat it. On the one hand, we told students not to worry about borrowing more. On the other, we told universities students would become much more demanding.

Both claims turned out to be half true. Full-time students were not put off by extra debt, but the number of part-time students fell sharply and has yet to recover. Universities found students had clearer expectations, but change was incremental and more limited than we had envisaged.[3]

In a valedictory interview when he stood down as an MP, David Willetts, the former Universities and Science Minister who pushed the

2012 reforms through, said teaching quality was 'unfinished business' and that 'teaching has been by far the weakest aspect of English higher education'.[4]

Our work at the Higher Education Policy Institute (HEPI), much of it undertaken in conjunction with the Higher Education Academy (HEA), supports this. The annual Student Academic Experience Survey began in 2006 as a way of monitoring what happens when you raise fees. The latest wave confirms that students still work less hard than the Quality Assurance Agency say they should.[5]

Our work has contributed to the debate in other ways too. For example, another recent joint HEPI / HEA survey confirms earlier evidence that international students may work harder than home ones. Over half of respondents said international students work either 'much harder' (22 per cent) or 'a little harder' (32 per cent) than home students, while only a tiny proportion said international students work either 'less hard' (3 per cent) or 'much less hard' (1 per cent).[6]

This suggests there is room for improvement and the renewed focus on teaching quality and student engagement is welcome. But the devil is in the detail, particularly for the forthcoming Teaching Excellence Framework (TEF). Jo Johnson, the Universities and Science Minister, has promised it will be 'proportionate and light touch, not big, bossy and bureaucratic.'[7]

The sector must hold policymakers to that, but the TEF also needs to be flexible enough to recognise there is no one-size-fits-all model of good teaching in higher education. It can occur on intensive employment-focused courses at newer universities or via distance learning programmes informed by smart data analytics or in small tutorials undertaken amidst ivory towers.

It would be a tragedy if the TEF went off at half-cock because it was devised in a rush. We must not repeat the failure of performance-related pay for schoolteachers. When that was introduced at the turn of the century, most teachers applied and most passed. It was bureaucratic and ineffective. Getting the TEF right by absorbing all we know about what works in the classroom is more important than getting it in place quickly.[8] At an institutional level, success is likely to depend on smart leadership that aims to secure the full engagement of staff. That cannot be delivered overnight either. Like the old Guinness advert, we need to remember that 'good things come to those who wait'.

Although the TEF is expected to be a basket of different measures, it remains fashionable to question the value of contact hours and class size as indicators. They do need careful handling but they should not be ignored. Graham Gibbs says 'class size predicts student performance' and, while he has persuasively criticised simplistic measures of contact hours, he has also found 'some pedagogic systems use class contact in ways that are very much more effective than others'.[9] We must listen to students too, who according to our surveys are less content when they have fewer contact hours and larger classes. Contact hours and class size are far from a catch-all, but they do matter when assessed together and in the round.

Expansion of higher education will continue, spurred on by the removal of student number controls. Indeed, in terms of the future shape of the sector, the removal of student number controls could be a more important policy than the tripling of tuition fees. We need to think deeply about the challenges that presents. The last half a century has comprehensively disproved Kingsley Amis's lament that 'MORE WILL MEAN WORSE' but more does mean different.[10]

In particular, it means thinking about the challenges faced by first-year students making the jump to university-level study. In his 2015 HEPI Annual Lecture, Professor Paul Wellings, Vice-Chancellor of Wollongong University, noted Australian universities are 'encouraging the use of specialist staff with high level skills in first year teaching.'[11] Yet this has not been enough to hold down a surge in non-continuation rates, with one recent Australian newspaper headline warning 'Drop-outs soar as unis ride enrolment boom'.[12]

The challenges of expansion are often regarded as of most concern to researchers who fear more competition for the available resources. But they are a key concern for leaders of teaching and learning too, and are not just in the classroom. They affect other areas of student life too and these can have knock-on consequences for learning. For example, students report lower wellbeing than others, which suggests there is a need to improve student support services, including counselling and mental health services, despite the challenging financial times.[13]

Perhaps the ultimate goal of the renewed focus on teaching and learning should be the ability to say with confidence that, if the international league tables were to start measuring teaching as effectively as they do research, the UK would perform as well as it does already.

The plural of anecdote is not evidence, but I hope I will be forgiven for ending on a second personal note. As a former teacher, I welcome the current focus on teaching quality in HE because I know firsthand how critical imparting knowledge and skills to others is for the future. Some might say the rewards are more intense, more immediate and more frequent than for those specialising in research, even if the financial emoluments and prestige are often lower. Good leadership can help ensure that is more widely understood.

Nick Hillman, Director of the Higher Education Policy Institute

# NOTES

1  Hillman, N. (2012) 'From grants for all to loans for all: Undergraduate finance from the implementation of the Anderson Report (1962) to the implementation of the Browne Report (2012)', *Contemporary British History*, 27(3): 249–270.

2  Cowley, P. (2005) 'Not mission impossible but mission bloody difficult', *The Rebels: How Blair mislaid his majority*, London: Politico's Publishing Ltd (173–205).

3  For some examples of changes that did occur, see the contributions to Nick Hillman (ed.) *'What do I get?': Ten essays on students fees, student choice and student engagement*. HEPI, February 2015.

4  Gill, J. (2015) *David Willetts interview: 'What I did was in the interests of young people'*. Available from www.timeshighereducation.co.uk/david-willetts-what-i-did-was-in-the-interests-of-young-people (accessed 7 September 2015).

5  Buckley, A., Soilemetzidis, I. and Hillman, N. (2015) *The 2015 Student Academic Experience Survey*, HEPI/HEA (p. 23). Available from www.hepi.ac.uk/wp-content/uploads/2015/06/AS-PRINTED-HEA_HEPI_report_print4.pdf (accessed 7 September 2015).

6  The balance is made up by those who think international students work the same as home students (33%) and by don't knows (9%). Hillman, N. (2015) *What do home students think of studying with international students?*, HEPI Report 76, (p. 3). Available from www.hepi.ac.uk/wp-content/uploads/2015/06/HEApaper7_web.pdf (accessed 9 September 2015).

7  Johnson, J. 'Teaching at the heart of the system', Speech to UniversitiesUK, 1 July 2015. Available from www.gov.uk/government/speeches/teaching-at-the-heart-of-the-system (accessed 9 September 2015).

8  Hillman, N. 'What's the gestation of a TEF?', *HEPI blog*, 19 August 2015. Available from www.hepi.ac.uk/2015/08/28/whats-gestation-period-tef/ (accessed 9 September 2015).

9  Gibbs, G. (2010) *Dimensions of quality*. York: Higher Education Academy (p. 15 and p. 21).

10 Amis, K. (1960) 'Lone voices: Views of the "fifties"', *Encounter*, as reprinted in Silver, H. (2003) *Higher education and opinion making in twentieth-century England*, London: Routledge (p. 179).

11 Wellings, P. (2014) *The architecture and the plumbing: What features do the Higher Education systems in the UK and Australia have in common?*, HEPI Annual Lecture (p. 5). Available from www.hepi.ac.uk/wp-content/uploads/2014/11/FINAL-PUBLISHED-VERSION.pdf (accessed 9 September 2015).

12 Hare, J. (2015) 'Drop-outs soar as unis ride enrolment boom', *The Australian*, 3 August 2015. Available from www.theaustralian.com.au/higher-education/drop-outs-soar-as-unis-ride-enrolment-boom/story-e6frgcjx-1227467093509?sv=41d8c05be3451174d84c0cca3b2e7611 (accessed 9 September 2015).

13 Hillman, N. (2015) *The HEPI-HEA 2015 Student Academic Experience Survey: Summary and recommendations*, HEPI and the HEA. Available from www.hepi.ac.uk/wp-content/uploads/2015/06/AS-PRINTED-HEA_Student-Academic-Experiance-Survey-Report_PRINT3.pdf (accessed 9 September 2015).

# Glossary

**4\* journal article**   with reference to the Research Excellence Initiative, a journal publication deemed to be world-leading.

**ACE Programme**   the American Council of Education offers programmes for new deans and chairs of schools, to assist with a number of the practical day-to-day issues.

**Affirmative action**   positive discrimination in favour of disadvantaged groups.

**Appreciative inquiry (AI)**   a change management tool or model which focuses on identifying what is working well, analysing why it is working well, then building on this foundation.

**Apprenticeships**   work/skills-based programmes, with apprentices earning whilst they are learning. Sometimes called 'day release', apprenticeships are based in the work place and the mode of learning is a blended, ongoing process.

**Aurora Programme**   a female only programme offered by the Leadership Foundation (LFHE) in the UK, to develop the 'leaky pipeline' in career progression in HE.

**Australian Learning and Teaching Council (ALTC)**   a national organisation with a mission to enhance learning and teaching in Australian higher education. It was replaced by the Office for Learning and Teaching.

**Blended learning**   using a mixture of approaches: face-to-face, small group, online, self-directed, etc.

**Board**   a term for the governing body of a university, e.g. the board of governors, the board of trustees.

**Carpe Diem**   'seize the day', so a useful name for short, sharp, focused workshops.

**Charter for Good Teaching**   agreement between teaching staff and students as to what constitutes 'good teaching', with responsibilities on both sides.

**Collective responsibility**   a key term for executive team members. Further to post-debate and discussion, whatever the final decision, everyone commits to stand by the decision with no further dissention.

**Contingency planning**   going through 'what if' scenarios, determining what the course of action will need to be if there is deviation from the key steps of the masterplan (part of risk mitigation).

**Council**   another term for the board; the body responsible for the governance of a university.

**Council of University Chairs (CUC)**   the body to which university chairs belong. In a sense, the professional group for chairs, commissioning appropriate research and resources, and offering training for the various roles of chairs and other members of governing bodies.

**Coursera**   an education platform which partners with top universities globally to offer free online courses, including MOOCs.

**Creative Skillset**   The industry lead body for the creative industries.

**Cultural anatomy model**   devised by Marshall (2007), it draws on the work of McKinsey's 7S model of hard and soft skills, with 'values' being the 'glue' in terms of analysing an organisation's culture in order to evaluate its readiness to change.

**Cultural framework**   determining the framework which best sums up the culture of an organisation or 'the way things are done around here'.

**Culture change**   bringing about a change in behaviours, dependent on shared values and analysis as to how to achieve the shared vision and shared objectives.

**Dearing (1997)**   the report of the National Committee of Inquiry into HE. The largest review of HE in the UK since the Robbins review of the early 1960s. The most significant change recommended was the shift in funding from a wholly state-funded system of grants for students, to a mixed system which included tuition fees.

**Degree classifications**   the grading system for undergraduate programmes in the UK: 1st, 2:1, 2:2, 3rd and ordinary degrees.

**Department for Business, Innovation and Skills (BIS)**   the UK government department which has responsibility for universities and higher education.

**Differential attainment**   variations in the educational attainment between students according to, for example, their social class or ethnic background.

**Digital literacy** skill and adeptness at engaging with a range of technological sources.

**edX** a platform for offering online courses and content, including MOOCs. Also undertakes research to explore how technology can transform learning. The platform includes courses from MIT, Harvard, Berkeley, etc.

**Entrance tariffs** the grades or points that post-16 students need to gain for entry to HE.

**eText** 'electronic text': a general term for any document that is read in digital form.

**EU Treaty of Amsterdam** (1997) emphasises citizenship and the rights of individuals, with increased powers for the European Parliament.

**Excellence initiative** a funding initiative introduced in Germany firstly, to address preconditions for excellence in research, and more recently, to address preconditions for excellence in teaching.

**FutureLearn** a private company wholly owned by the Open University, offering distance and online learning (to include MOOCs) globally. Many of the partners in this venture are the best UK and international universities.

**Gender mainstreaming** is a process of assessing the implications for both men and women of any planned action, and assessing what behavioural and organisational changes might be required to effectively mainstream proper representation.

**Ghettoisation** students from different backgrounds gravitating to each other, and ensuring that they live together, eat together, etc. thereby not gaining the benefits of cross-cultural exchange.

**Globalisation** the embedding of cultural perspectives in the education of the student, to include the curriculum.

**Graduate attributes** the range of attributes that a graduate will explore over and beyond the discipline-specific educational programme they study, such as team working, global citzenship, critical thinking.

**Guiding coalition** a group of staff with status and power who group together to lead and manage change.

**HEA/HEPI Student Academic Experience Survey** a survey conducted jointly by the Higher Education Academy and the Higher Education Policy Institute looking at all relevant aspects of UK HE student academic experience, providing important metrics for HEIs.

**HEFCE** Higher Education Funding Council for England

**HERDSA** the Higher Education Research and Development Society of Australasia.

**HETL**   the Higher Education Teaching and Learning portal.

**Higher Education Academy (HEA)**   a sector agency in the UK, set up in 2004 to support the professionalisation of teaching staff in higher education.

**Higher Education Authority**   the funding authority in Ireland with responsibility for higher education.

**IBM**   a bluechip American technology and consulting company (International Business Machines); undertakes research into innovative use of technology to enhance communications and learning.

**ISSOTL**   International Society for the Scholarship of Teaching and Learning

**Jarratt Report (1985)**   a Committee of Vice-Chancellors and Principals (CVCP) commissioned report into HE, which heralded the introduction of 'managerialism' in universities in that it flagged up the need for dedicated managers.

**JISC**   formerly the Joint Infrastructure Systems Committee, a UK sector agency with responsibility for supporting the HE sector with educational technology initiatives.

**Key performance indicators (KPIs)**   a metric which can be monitored to determine progress towards a particular business goal, which similarly has a metric attached.

**Khan Academy**   a non-profit educational body set up in 2006 in the US, offering online courseware (credited with being the first to offer MOOCs) to provide greater access to high-quality educational resources.

**Kübler-Ross transition curve**   a change management tool, originally developed by Elisabeth Kübler-Ross in the 1960s to explain the emotional stages of the grieving process. Likening any 'change' to the grieving process – ie the need to 'let go' and move on, this model is a helpful tool when planning for the potential impact of change on different staff.

**Leadership Foundation for Higher Education (LF/LFHE)**   a UK sector agency set up in 2004 to support leaders, managers and governors in HE via research, networks, developmental programmes and masterclass.

**Learning (or learner) analytics**   a data-mining process which measures, collects and analyses different aspects of students' learning journey, for example, exploring accessing the library or viewing of online lectures, thereby aiding greater understanding of student engagement and progress.

**Learning and teaching hub**   with the advances in technology, 'hubs' have been set up to incorporate libraries, social space, group work space so that they become hubs for teaching and learning.

**Learning gain**   a means of assessing students' learning outcomes as a measure of distance travelled from entry into HE through to employment.

**Learning hubs**   technologically enabled accommodation, including high-speed wifi for individual student and group work activity.

**Lecture capture**   the recording of lectures for the virtual learning environment (VLE), so that students can either watch the lecture again, rewinding portions that they have not understood, or can watch for the first time if they were unable to attend at the scheduled lecture time.

**Lifestyle lectures**   the introduction of lectures which meet with students' learning styles and preferences for learning. From a data bank, software will detect which lectures best suit their lifestyle, thereby personalising their learning.

**MBTI**   Myers Briggs Type Inventory. A theory of different personality types, based on the theory of Jung. Using a psychometric questionnaire, measuring psychological preference, a four letter 'type' is generated, providing useful insights into such things as one's preferred decision-making process.

**Measure learning**   attempts to determine which metrics might be used to chart the learners' journey through HE, gaining insights into which activities bring about the greatest learning.

**Mentoring and coaching**   two personal development techniques, the first via an experienced, more senior individual, who assists the mentee to consider what steps they need to take to progress their career; the second offering a sounding board to explore how one might make progress through examining goals, reality, opportunities and measures.

**MOOCs**   massive online, open courseware offered free across the globe. Creatively used for a range of purposes, to include engaging more potential higher education students with programmes which could assist them to transition into HE, through to courses which are of interest to the general public and existing students.

**National Forum for the Enhancement of Teaching and Learning**   the national body set up by the Irish Minister for Education and Skills. Reporting to the Higher Education Authority, it undertakes a similar role to that of the HEA in the UK, i.e. promoting the professionalisation of HE teaching staff.

**National Project Toward Building World Class Universities**   policy initiative in South Korea to assist universities to become more competitive and position the country to compete globally.

**National Student Survey of Engagement (NSSE)**   developed in the late 1990s, the NSSE is a survey which explores firstly, the amount of time and effort that students put in to their studies and related educational activity. It also explores how the HEI deploys its resources, organises its curriculum and other educational opportunities to facilitate student engagement. Adapted to be culturally aligned in the UK, the UK Engagement Survey (UKES) draws heavily on the approach used in the US.

**Nolan Principles**   derived from the UK Report of the Committee for Standards in Public Life, the principles are the basis of the ethical standards expected of holders of public office. The principles are: selflessness, integrity, objectivity, accountability, openness, honesty and leadership.

**National Student Survey (NSS)**   a UK annual survey which gathers students' opinions on the quality of their courses. The purpose is to provide public accountability as the results are converted into well-publicised league tables and provide information which can assist prospective students in making informed choices.

**Office for Learning and Teaching (OLT)**   set up by the Australian Government to encourage best practice in institutional change that enhances teaching and learning. It has just received notice that its funding is not to be renewed.

**Organisational culture**   often said to be 'the way we do things around here', i.e. the skills, behaviours and attitudes which determine the outcomes of processes and projects.

**Pearson**   a global publisher which additionally is now a provider of 'learning solutions', to include resources and assessment tools.

**Peer review**   the assessment process of a piece of work carried out by one's peers, i.e. those in a similar line of work who have the recognised competence to make a valid judgement.

**Pre-92**   a term now increasingly less used in the UK, refers to the HEIs whose title was changed to 'university' as a result of the Further and Higher Education Act (1992).

**Primus inter pares**   'first amongst equals'; a leadership approach whereby the leader works collectively with their team, engaging staff in decision-making and action without deploying positional power or authority.

**Professional bodies**   non-profit organisations which act in the interests of both the profession and the members they serve, ultimately for the public interest.

**Progression data**   tracking the performance of students through online monitoring systems so that progress can be monitored, with appropriate interventions being made if they are thought to be helpful.

**Psychological contract**   deemed far more binding than the employment contract by many, the underpinning understanding of what it is the employee gets out of the organisation beyond the contract (e.g. exceptional work colleagues) and what it is the organisation gets out of the employee beyond someone fulfilling their job description (e.g. wonderful ambassador for the university).

**PVC network**   a voluntary network, which coordinates the 150+ pro-vice-chancellors (or vice-presidents or vice-principals), to act in their interest, via regular virtual and face-to-face meetings.

**QA regime**   refers to the translation of the national quality assurance system at the higher education institutional level.

**QAA**   the Quality Assurance Agency, in the UK.

**RACI**   a management tool, which is also referred to as the 'responsibility assignment matrix' as it identifies: responsible person, accountabilities, consultation processes, and information flow.

**Reflective practice**   the process of quiet contemplation over one's practice, primarily after the event, considering 'what worked well, what not so well, what would I do differently next time' – i.e. what was learned.

**Regulatory frameworks**   necessary regulations (to include legislation) that an organisation needs to take account of and address. Often this requires the following of certain procedures or practices.

**Research Excellence Framework (REF)**   introduced for the first time in the UK in 2014 to replace the Research Assessment Exercise, it assesses the quality of research in UK HEIs.

**Risk Assessment**   a systematic analysis of a process, project or intervention to identify the potential for derailment, negative consequences or non-compliance with set policies and procedures.

**Sandpit of creativity**   the recognition that creativity often stems from play (look at children and the imaginative outputs of their play, the sandpit being a great example).

**Scholarly and service activities**   exploring the impact of educational activities such as research into one's own teaching practice, or reaching out into the community by providing service activity.

**Scival system**   an expert profiling and research networking tool which, for example, provides a citation and abstract database.

**SEDA**   Staff and Educational Development Association.

**Shadowing**   working alongside someone to learn from their practice and expertise.

**Snowball approach** a management term which suggests starting a change project by working with a pilot of on-message participants, gathering more support when the change initiative demonstrates success and gaining momentum as the number of people engaged becomes larger and larger as time progresses.

**SOTL** the Scholarship of Teaching and Learning.

**Spellings Commission** (2005) a US federal government committee set up to explore why so many tertiary education students were not deriving the benefits from tertiary education – either in financial or academic terms – as they should.

**SRHE** the Society for Research into Higher Education.

**Stakeholder mapping** a management technique which requires mapping out stakeholders in terms of power and interestedness, and considering which groups or individuals fall into the different categories, so as to determine a communications strategy to get (and keep) key groups on side.

**Student app** along with social media, the relevant apps to enhance students' engagement with the learning environment.

**Teaching Excellence Framework (TEF)** to be introduced by the English government in 2016. An initiative to bring about parity of esteem with the REF, to provide greater focus on excellent student outcomes, and to provide value for money for students.

**Town Hall meetings** meetings of all staff in which the executive provides 'state of the nation' reports, announce changes, and take questions in an open forum.

**UCEA** the Universities and Colleges Employment Association.

**Udacity** an online platform for MOOCs.

**Unbundled and rebundled** terms for examining the blended learning approach, unbundling the present offer and determining whether or not the balance of online and other is correct for the different student needs.

**UTS Model of Learning** the distinctive approach and term coined by the University of Technology, Sydney, Australia.

**Virtual engagement** engagement via online and social media, rather than face-to-face.

**Virtual learning environment (VLE)** the platform used by universities to provide online support for all programmes of study. There is likely to be a pan-university VLE, with a range of information for students, and also programme-specific restricted sites for enrolled students, where course information, resources, etc. are provided.

**VP (Teaching and Learning)**   a generic title used to cover pro-vice-chancellors (PVCs), deputy-vice-chancellors (DVCs), vice-principals (VPs) or vice-presidents (VPs) holding portfolio responsibility for teaching and learning.

**Which?**   a UK publication aimed at consumers, which focuses on exploring quality and value for money.

**Wicked issues**   challenging global issues which require a range of interdisciplinary expertise to unpack and seek possible solutions to, for example, global warming, 'aging', conflict.

**YouGov/Guardian poll**   polls of public perceptions regularly conducted to ascertain the public's views on a range of topics.

# Index